THE CAVE HUNTERS

Biographical sketches of the lives of

Sir William Boyd Dawkins
(1837-1929)
and
Dr. J. Wilfrid Jackson
(1880-1978)

EDITED BY M. J. BISHOP

Published by the Derbyshire Museum Service

ISBN 0 906753 02 3

EDITOR'S INTRODUCTION

This booklet was produced in the first instance to accompany the exhibition on the life and work of Sir William Boyd Dawkins and Dr. J. Wilfrid Jackson held at Buxton Museum in 1982, and also commemorates the opening on 21st May 1982 of the Boyd Dawkins Room by Dr. Derek Roe. The Boyd Dawkins Room, which is actually dedicated to both Dawkins and Jackson, is a period style study room (circa 1900) housing the library of Sir William Boyd Dawkins and featuring many items such as pictures, ornaments and furniture that once graced his own study.

Both Sir William and Dr. Jackson were attached to the Museum in Manchester University for much of their lives, so it is unusual, but very fortunate for Buxton, that Buxton Museum should be chosen as the home for their respective libraries, scientific manuscripts, correspondence, and personalia. The story must be taken back to 1928 when Sir William Boyd Dawkins opened the new Buxton Museum and Public Library. Sir William had a soft spot for the Peak District which represented so many of his interests in its geology and archaeology, and in particular its bone caves, so he was only too anxious to see a small provincial museum which covered his own interests make a good start in the world. Sir William died in 1929, and following his instructions his widow Lady Mary Boyd Dawkins donated his library and manuscripts to the Museum, and a Boyd Dawkins Reference Room was opened in 1929 by Sir Arthur Keith, Sir Arthur Evans and Professor Sayce. The collection after the war was moved to various parts of the building until it finally ended up in the store-rooms, but upon the Derbyshire County Museum Service taking over the present premises in 1975 all the available Museum space has been placed under redevelopment, of which the opening of the Boyd Dawkins Room is one phase.

Bringing the story up to date, Buxton Museum has been doubly fortunate in acquiring the library, scientific manuscripts, correspondence, and personalia of Dr. J. Wilfrid Jackson who retired to Buxton in 1945 and who died in 1978. Dr. Jackson was not only a close colleague of Sir William but followed many of his research interests, so the Museum now holds a scientific archive of just two men working in the same fields covering over a hundred years. Dr. Jackson was for many years an Honorary Consultant to Buxton Museum, and it is much to be regretted that he never lived to see the first phases of its redevelopment. His daughter, Miss A. S. Jackson has been exceedingly generous in donating many of Dr. Jackson's papers to the Museum, and has allowed the present writer many opportunities to visit her to sort through her father's papers and consult personal diaries and archives.

The biographical sketch of Sir William Boyd Dawkins was written by Dr. Jackson and appeared in the journal Cave Science in 1966, and the Derbyshire Museum Service is grateful to the British Cave Research Association for permission to reprint this article. The only changes to Dr. Jackson's paper are the addition of a number of papers in the bibliography and the addition of several photographs.

My own contribution on Dr. Jackson largely derives from the many manuscript notes made by him, from newspaper cuttings and published papers, and from his diaries, all of which Miss A. S. Jackson kindly gave me access to. Miss Jackson also imparted to me many reminiscences of her father's active career, and kindly read through my manuscript. The present writer has come into contact with many friends and colleagues of Dr. Jackson, but much to my disappointment never met him. My biographical sketch of his life had to be put together in only a few months, and included no personal knowledge, so I offer this biography as just a preliminary appreciation of his life and work. In the enormous archive that now exists in Buxton Museum on both Sir William Boyd Dawkins and Dr. Jackson, there are many opportunities for biographical and scientific research on the development of studies in prehistory and geology between 1860 and 1960 in particular.

After Miss Jackson's most kind help, I must also extend thanks to Dr. R. M. C. Eagar of Manchester University for access to the notebooks and diaries of Sir William Boyd Dawkins, to the late Mr. Samuel Taylor (the nephew by marriage of Sir William's daughter Ella) who very kindly supplied several photographs of Sir William and his family, and to the staff of the Derbyshire Museum Service for their help in the production of this booklet.

M. J. Bishop
Curator, Buxton Museum.
March, 1982

MUSEUMS WITH MAJOR COLLECTIONS OF DAWKINS & JACKSON MATERIAL

COLLECTOR	MUSEUM	MATERIAL
Dawkins	Buxton Museum	Library, archives, & some antiquities, fossils & furniture
Jackson	Buxton Museum	Library, archives, Derbyshire Carboniferous fossils
Dawkins	Manchester Museum	Fossil & Archaeological collections, & some archives
Jackson	Manchester Museum	Fossil & Archaeological collections, & some archives
Dawkins	Manchester City Art Gallery	Furniture, paintings, cloisonée enamels
Jackson	Merseyside Museums, Liverpool	Conchology and fossils
Jackson	British Museum (Natural History)	Tertiary & Recent Brachiopods
Dawkins	British Museum (Natural History)	Pleistocence mammals

SIR WILLIAM BOYD DAWKINS (1837-1929)

A Biographical Sketch

By J. Wilfrid Jackson, D.Sc., F.S.A., F.G.S.

This biography has been compiled from many sources including the obituaries by Sir Arthur Smith Woodward and Professor F. E. Weiss in journals and newspapers (Guardian, Evening News, and City News), from Dawkins publications, and from personal reminiscences. I was acquainted with Dawkins and worked under his supervision at the Manchester Museum for some 22 years and attended his lectures before my appointment as Curator in 1907. During my tenure at the museum I received great help from him in arranging and classifying the geological collections.

William Boyd Dawkins was the son of the Rev. Richard Dawkins and was born at Buttington Vicarage, Welshpool, on the 26th of December 1837. He died at his home, Richmond Lodge, Bowdon, Cheshire, on the 15th of January, 1929, in his 92nd year. The funeral service was held at Holy Innocents Church, Fallowfield, Manchester, and was conducted by the rector, the Rev. H. D. Lockett, and the Rev. Samuel Taylor (son-in-law), vicar of Holy Trinity, Carlisle. The committal was at the Manchester Crematorium.

Dawkins received his early education at the well-known public school of Rossall, near Fleetwood, Lancashire (opened in 1844 by the then Head Master, the Rev. Dr. John Woolley). This school was founded for the 8 to 15 years old sons of clergymen of the Estabished Church. Dawkins became one of Rossall's eminent sons. Later he went to Jesus College, Oxford, where he

Rossall School, Fleetwood, in 1857. Etching supplied by Rossall School.

distinguished himself in classics and in natural sciences; he graduated in 1860. It was at Oxford that, under the influence of Professor John Phillips, he became an enthusiastic geologist.

Buttington Church, near Welshpool. Dawkins' father was vicar of this church, and Dawkins was born in Buttington Vicarage, 1837. Photo: Manchester Museum.

As an undergraduate at Oxford he came in contact with J. R. Green, who later became the historian. They found that both were interested in the relation of geology to history. Green resolved to deal with the history of Britain in the written record and Dawkins took over the prehistory as revealed by geology and archaeology.

The exploration of Kent's Hole, Torquay, by William Pengelly and others, led Dawkins, as a young undergraduate at Oxford, to turn his attention to cave research. In December 1859 he began the excavation of the hyaena den at Wookey Hole, near Wells, Somerset, with the Rev. J. Williamson, and found Palaeolithic implements of Mousterian type associated with the remains of many extinct Pleistocene animals. In later years he was joined in work by Willett, Parker and Sanford. Full reports of the exploration were published by Dawkins in 1862 and 1863. He was then B.A.Oxon, and a Fellow of the Geological Society of London. The hyaena den was his first cave and his work there led to his connection with the Somersetshire Archaeological and Natural History Society. He attended his first meeting in 1862 and never lost contact with the county. He became President in 1912 and often spoke of being a Somerset man by adoption.

In 1861, at the age of twenty four,

Mr. & Mrs. W. Boyd Dawkins' Wedding Breakfast, 26th July, 1866. Pen and Ink Sketch: Manchester Museum.

Frances Boyd Dawkins, née Frances Evans the daughter of Robert Speke Evans, Clerk to the Admiralty, and Dawkins' first wife. She died in 1921. Photo: Mr. S. Taylor, J.P.

Ella Selina Boyd Dawkins, the Dawkins's only child. She married the Rev. Samuel Taylor in 1915 and died in 1969.
Photo: Mr. S. Taylor, J.P.

Dawkins was appointed to the Geological Survey of Great Britain and became a junior colleague of Huxley in Jermyn Street Museum, London. For eight years he was occupied in mapping the Wealden and other formations in Kent and the Thames Valley. In this work he developed a keen interest in the mammalian remains of the river gravels which led to the publication of numerous memoirs and papers dealing with the same. It is impossible to deal with more than a selection of these. In addition to Wookey Hole already mentioned Dawkins with the assistance of Sanford explored a cavern of the prehistoric age in Burrington Combe. This yielded large numbers of remains of domestic animals and other objects. This was in 1863. In that year he pubished an important paper on the dentition of *Rhinoceros tichorhinus* (Woolly rhinoceros) and in 1865 papers on the dentition of *Rhinoceros megarhinus* and *Hyaena spelaea*. He was then M.A.Oxon. These papers were well illustrated and his footnotes show that this author was familiar with the British and Continental literature. In 1864 he published an account of the discovery of the earliest British fossil mammal, found at Watchet, Somerset, to which he gave the name *Hypsiprymnopsis rhaeticus*. It is probably a marsupial related to the Kangaroo-rats of Australia.

Dawkins was elected a Fellow of the Royal Society in 1866 and in that year he married Frances Evans by whom he had a daughter Ella Selina. Mrs. Dawkins died in 1921 and in May 1922 Dawkins married Mary, the widow of Hubert Congreve. The daughter married the Rev. Samuel Taylor, then rector of Holy Innocents Church, Fallowfield, Manchester, and later vicar of Holy Trinity Church, Carlisle.

In 1866 also began the publication of British Pleistocene Mammalia (Pal.Soc.) by Dawkins in which he was assisted by W. Ashford Sanford. This was a most important work and dealt with the cave-lion which Dawkins maintained was identical with the existing lion. This joint work continued until 1872. Other papers followed in 1866 including one on 'The Habits and Conditions of the Two earliest-known Races of Men', and one on 'The Pleistocene Mammals of Yorkshire'. In 1867 Dawkins gave an address at the opening of the Blackmore Museum, Salisbury on 'The Pre-historical Mammalia found associated with Man in Great Britain'. In the same year came papers on 'The Dentition of *Rhinoceros leptorhinus'*; one on 'The Age of the Lower Brick-earths of the Thames Valley', and one on the discovery of remains of the Arctic animal known as the Musk-Ox in Britain; this was followed by further papers on this animal in 1872, 1883 and 1885. In 1868 Dawkins published his views on the former range of the mammoth and of the reindeer in Europe, and in the same year dealt with the dentition of *Rhinoceros etruscus*.

In 1869 came a change in Dawkins' life. On the recommendation of Huxley he was appointed curator of the natural history collections at the old Manchester Museum, in Peter Street (on the site of the present Y.M.C.A. building). The museum was founded in 1821 and Dawkins' task was a formidable one. He had gained some experience of curatorial work in his early days at the Museum of Practical Geology, London, with Huxley. The material at Manchester consisted of a general collection of natural history specimens accumulated by the Manchester Natural History Society (founded 1821) and a large and important geological collection from the Manchester Geological Society (founded 1838). The general collection had been under the care of several curators, 1821-1835 Thomas Hewitt: 1836-1838, W. C. Williamson: 1838-1862, Captain Thomas Brown: 1862-1868, Thomas Alcock, and the geological material had been looked after by Binney, Ormerod, and others. In the course of time most specimens, especially insects and birds, had deteriorated and many had to be destroyed. The geological material, from its nature, was in fairly good condition. Dawkins mentioned something about the condition of the collections in a President's Address to the Museums Association. He pointed out that the natural collection had been first class in its earlier days, but had ceased to grow, and therefore had become dead. The geological collection was in good order. Both, however, were in a deplorable state, so far as related to fittings, and were simply ignored by the general public, and scarcely used by students.

Dawkins' duties included lectures in geology at Owens College (founded 1851) then in Quay Street, Manchester (the former residence of Richard Cobden). He had the task of moving the collections from Peter Street to Quay Street, after some sorting had taken place. In 1872, when Williamson resigned the geological part of his professorship, Dawkins was appointed to succeed him as Professor of Geology. This added much to his duties.

In 1873 the collections were removed from Quay Street to new college premises in Oxford Road, Manchester, and for some time had to be stored in lower rooms and attics. Their removal caused some amusement among the public as the procession of stuffed animals passed along Oxford Road. The collection included an elephant and giraffe which on arrival at their destination were placed among the geological specimens on the ground floor because they could not be got up the stairs. Owing to its height the giraffe had to be laid on the top of one of the cases, and to keep it from dust it was swathed all over with calico. The elephant and giraffe were later removed to the Belle Vue Zoo.

Later, Owens College and the collections became incorporated in the new Victoria University (founded 1880). In 1888 a main museum building fronting Oxford Road was opened and Dawkins was able to arrange the specimens in proper order. His scientific arrangement proved a valuable basis for the later development of the Manchester Museum.

With the Museum and the University most of Dawkins active life was spent. He resigned the chair of geology in 1909, but remained connected with the Museum as scientific supervisor of the geological department and as a member of the Committee of Management. On his retirement from the University he was made honorary professor and received the honorary degree of doctor of science. He was knighted in 1919.

It might be mentioned here that in 1874 Dawkins was a candidate for the Professorship of Geology at Oxford in succession to the late Professor John Phillips. He had many excellent testimonials but was unsuccessful.

Unfortunately his 'Cave Hunting' book had not then been published but was in the press.

Dawkins negotiated many exchanges and donations for the Manchester Museum, and added much of his own material. In 1889 he presented a large collection of fossils from all formations and including the major part of the vertebrate and other remains obtained by him from caves and river gravels of the Pleistocene age. In May, 1874, he and a Mr. H. Wilde were taking a walk near the copper mines at Alderley Edge and they discovered a number of grooved stone hammers which had been used in the past for mining purposes. They had been made from glacial boulders. Most of them were presented to the museum.

Dawkins had come to Manchester fully equipped with knowledge of caving and in the ensuing years was soon involved, amongst his other activities, in cave investigations. He had made a special study of the mammalia of the Tertiary Period and had paid great attention to the problem connected with Early Man. Many caves and other habitation or burial places had already been explored by him. Much of the evidence acquired in this way was ably dealt with in his two well-known works, 'Cave Hunting', published in 1874, and 'Early Man in Britain', published in 1880. Both are very readable books and contain a wealth of important information. The first was written by Dawkins as Curator of the Museum and Lecturer in Geology in the Owens College, Manchester, and was dedicated by him to the Baroness Burdett Coutts, Founder of the scholarship in Geology at Oxford. He was her first scholar. In his preface Dawkins points out that since the year 1823, when Dr. Buckland published his famous work 'Reliquiae Diluvianae', no attempt had been made to correlate and bring into the compass of one work the crude mass of facts which had been recorded in nearly every country in Europe. In addition to much detailed information on the physical aspect of caves the author makes reference to very many British and Foreign caves which have yielded evidence of use by man as habitations and by animals as dens. He gives a good summary of his explorations at the Wookey Hole hyaena-den in 1859-60 and in addition sums up the results of the investigations of European and British caves, citing those of Yorkshire, Derbyshire, North and South Wales, the Mendips, and many others.

In his 1880 work Dawkins traced prehistoric trade-routes from the Mediterranean to Cornwall and the Baltic for tin and amber. He also discussed the origin and development of the Bronze Age civilisation, and advanced the theory that the Eskimos were the descendants of Upper Palaeolithic people, and the Picts and other elements in the population of North West Europe were the survivals from the Neolithic races.

It is impossible to deal here with the enormous amount of research carried out by Dawkins. his published papers and memoirs are very numerous and one wonders how he found time to write them, especially when he was dealing with the Old Manchester Museum among other matters. All that can be done is to make a judicious selection and point out some of the salient features.

William Boyd Dawkins, taken about 1870, when he had just taken up his appointment as Curator of the Natural History Collections in the Manchester Museum.
Photo: Buxton Museum.

Soon after Dawkins commenced his research he realised that far more study was needed in the case of the mammalian remains found in caves and other deposits. He made a point of visiting what collections were available, both in the British Isles and on the Continent, and made copious notes and drawings. He became particularly interested in the deer family and the course of evolution of the antlers. In a series of papers beginning in 1868, before he came to Manchester, he described a number of new species from the Forest Bed and Red Crag of East Anglia. One species was named after him in 1880 by E. T. Newton, another worker in the same field.

In 1870 a British Association Committee was formed for the scientific investigation of the Victoria Cave, Settle, and Dawkins was soon employed in the identification of the animal remains and other objects met with during the research. He was responsible for the pubication of progress reports in 1870, 1871 and 1872, when R. H. Tiddeman took over, but Dawkins remained on the Committee. A fair summary of the discoveries at Victoria Cave is to be found in the Proceedings of the British Speleological Association for September 1964, No. 2.

Dawkins had several acrimonious discussions in connection with cave excavations and this led to much publicity in the Press. There was much bitter feeling as to who first discovered Windy Knoll Fissure, near Castleton, Derbyshire. The first actual printed record was by J. Plant, of the Salford Museum, who, in 1874, published an article on the discovery of Pleistocene animal remains at the Fissure. The bones in question had been collected by two young men from Manchester, H. H. Hindshaw and E. Ramsbottom, in April, 1874, and brought to Plant who asked Dawkins for his opinion on them. They consisted of the bones of bison and reindeer. The publication of this discovery in public press aroused a good deal of feeling among certain people and led to other papers being published. In one of these, in May, 1875, Rooke Pennington, LL.B. solicitor of Bolton, put in a claim to having met with bones as early as October 1870 on a visit to Windy Knoll, and submitting several to Dawkins who pronounced them to belong to the urus and to be of Pleistocene age. Much of the argument is to be found in Pennington's book 'Notes on the Barrows and Bone-Caves of Derbyshire', 1877. This book, by the way, is dedicated to William Boyd Dawkins. John Tym and others of Castleton were involved in the argument. Plant, in a paper published in June 1875, doubted whether Dawkins had known of this supposed early discovery by Pennington as he makes no special reference to it in his 'Cave Hunting', 1874. All that is given is a short paragraph in 'Additions' on p.XXIV, calling attention to the ossiferous fissure at Windy Knoll, recently exported by Tym, Pennington, Plant, Walker and others.

It is difficult to account for this omission especially when one finds that Dawkins, in a published paper of May 1875, mentions that the first intimation he had of the presence of fossil mammalia at Windy Knoll was in October, 1870, when Pennington brought him part of a tibia and other bones thought at the time to belong to urus.

The number of limb bones of animals found ultimately at Windy Knoll amounted to no less than 1183 (exclusive of splinters) and of teeth and jaws no 429. They were classified by Dawkins as those of bison, reindeer, grisly bear, wolf, fox and hare. There was no trace of hyaena, nor of elephant or rhinoceros. The remains had evidently been washed in over a long period of time. A large collection is in the Manchester Museum.

In 1875, Dawkins linked up with the Rev. J. Magens Mello, Rector of St. Thomas' Church, New Brampton, Chesterfield, who had become interested in the caves of the Creswell Crags, near Worksop. The two worked together for several years and made some important discoveries, but space cannot be spared to give details here. The whole matter will be fully dealt with in the near future as 'The Story of the Creswell Caves'. What might be mentioned here is that four main caves were investigated by Dawkins and his colleagues. These were Pin Hole (partly), Robin Hood, Mother Grundy's Parlour, on the Derbyshire side of the ravine, and Church Hole, on the Nottinghamshire side. The careful investigations resulted in the establishment of a definite sequence of faunas and human races. The remains of hippopotamus, leptorhine rhinoceros and hyaena, were met with in the deeper levels of Mother Grundy's Parlour, but no traces of man or of mammoth or reindeer. These were discovered in the higher levels. This cave and the others were proved to have been used by hyaenas as dens at times and as shelters by Paleolithic hunters. At least two cultural levels were distinguished, a lower one with rudely chipped quartzite implements and an upper one with flint implements of the later Palaeolithic type accompanied with implements of bone and antler and an incised piece showing a horse's head.

the committee and obtained permission to work the caves from the Duke of Portland. I became a member of the cave committee and Dawkins said that I was to be responsible for the identification of the bones found.

Dawkins encouraged me in many ways both at the Manchester Museum and when I visited his home at Fallowfield and at Bowdon. On one such occasion, when discussing his book 'Cave Hunting' I asked him if he had ever thought of revising the work, he turned round and said he left it to me. I ultimately took on the archaeological side and the result is to be found in my chapter in 'British Caving' published by the Cave Research Group, in 1953 and 1962.

Water colour sketch of Creswell Crags, painted by the Rev. J. Magens Mello, 1876. Original: Manchester Museum.

Two of the Creswell caves were investigated in later years by members of the Derbyshire Cave Committee established in 1921 by the British Association acting jointly with the Royal Anthropological Institute, and the late A. Leslie Armstrong was entrusted with the conduct of the cave investigations. Dawkins was chairman of

Dawkins possessed remarkable skill in identifying fragmentary animal remains. In 1888 he critically examined a tooth found in the Red Crag of Suffolk and concluded that it belonged to an Indian type of racoon to which he gave the name *Ailurus anglicus*. According to Sir Arthur Smith Woodward (in 1931), the complete dentition was found later in rocks of the same age in Transylvania and this discovery showed that the animal was very closely allied to *Ailurus,* but was generically distinct.

In pursuit of knowledge he travelled to many places on the Continent and elsewhere. His most exciting adventures were in Australia and America. He used to talk to his friends and the Press about his trip to Australia where he had been sent as a consulting engineer to investigate and report on kerosene shale for a party of Manchester business men. He had been given power to pay any sum for the concession, but on close examination he found that the statements of the vendors were false and the whole thing was a fake. In fact the property did not belong to the men offering it for sale and a bribe of £8,000 was offered to Dawkins to cover up the forgery but this was scornfully refused. He went to Nevada during the silver boom and was given the chance of buying a silver mine for 350 dollars. On sampling the ore he found it was good, but he could not take on the mine without giving up his Manchester work. When in America he was offered, on his own terms, the headship of the University of California, but declined because he did not want to leave Manchester.

In Dawkins' later years economic geology claimed his attention, especially problems of water supply, and his name became closely associated with the proposed Channel Tunnel and the buried coal-field of S.E. England. The close identity of the coal-fields of Somerset and Bristol with those of North France and Belgium and the geological structure suggested that the same coal-bearing rocks would occur in S.E. England under a cover of newer formations. In evidence before a Royal Commission in 1871, two leading geologists, Godwen-Austen and Prestwich, clearly demonstrated that coal could be expected in Kent below a cover of newer rocks not likely to exceed 1000 to 2000 feet. Several borings were put down at different places but results were negative. To Dawkins belonged the honour of obtaining the first positive result. He suggested, in 1890, that a boring might be made at the bottom of the shaft sunk at the Dover end of the proposed tunnel. The boring was made and productive coal measures were met with at 1100 feet below O.D. This began the exploitation of the Kent Coalfield.

In 1898 he gave a lecture on 'The Relation of Geology to Engineering' — the James Forrest lecture — at the Institute of Civil Engineers, Westminster.

Dawkins was a popular lecturer at the Manchester Museum and elsewhere. This was well before the days of lantern slides and cine-films. In the Museum he used large diagrams pinned over the cases and his audiences stood around him. Some of these 'Science Lectures for the People' were delivered at The Hulme Town Hall, Manchester, and at the Publish Hall, Collyhurst, Manchester. There was one on 'Coal' at the first mentioned venue in 1870, and one on 'Our Earliest Ancestors in Britain' at the second place in 1879. These were printed off later and sold at one penny per copy. During the session 1889-90 he gave a course of eight lectures on the 'Ancient History of the Earth' at the Friends' Institute, Mount Street, Manchester, with demonstrations at the Manchester Museum on certain days. These lectures were in addition to his Geology and Palaeontology Courses and Physical Geography Lectures to students at the Owens College.

Dawkins was a member and at times President of many learned societies. He was a founder and the first President of the Lancashire and Cheshire Antiquarian Society and gave an address on 'The English Conquest of Britain', in 1883, and another on 'Lancashire and Cheshire in Prehistoric Times', in 1884. He was a member and past President of the Manchester Geological and Mining Society, a founder member of the Manchester Geographical Society, and Hon. Member of the Isle of Man Natural History and Antiquarian Society.

In 1903 Dawkins ended his own cave researches but still kept up his interest in the subject by giving advice on the renewed excavations at Creswell, and in other ways. In the above year he published an important paper on an ossiferous fissure at Dove Holes, near Buxton. The site was brought to his notice by Mr. Micah Salt, a well-known Buxton antiquary, who showed him some teeth which proved to be those of

Mastodon. They had been picked up by a boy of the name of Hick at the Victory Quarry, Dove Holes. The find led to a careful examination of the area and many more teeth and bones were found. These were identified by Dawkins as *Machairodus crenatidens* (sabre toothed tiger), *Hyaena* sp. *Mastodon arvernensis, Elephas meridionalis, Rhinoceros etruscus, Equus stenonis,* and *Cervus etueriarum* (?). The remains of these animals found in the limestone fissure were thought to have been washed down from a higher cave — a hyaena-den, in fact — and the teeth, bones and the accompanying stones and cave-earth had accumulated in the lower fissure. At the time of their discovery the age was given as Upper Pliocene, like similar remains from the Red Crag and Norwich Crag of East Anglia, but recent studies of the Crag deposits and analogous ones of the Continent has led workers to refer them to the Early (Basal) Pleistocene (i.e. Villafrankian) about the beginning of the First Glacial. This does not mean any real change in geological position, only a change of name. The Dove Holes discovery was regarded as of outstanding importance as the geology indicated that the region had suffered tremendous denudation. It was estimated that some 330 feet vertical thickness of limestone and other rocks had been removed.

Dawkins rarely had any fossil named after him, but in 1909 he was honoured by one of his old students, D. M. S. Watson (afterward Professor), who described and figured a fossil marine reptile from the Upper Lias of Whitby as *Sthenarosaurus dawkinsi.*

In addition to his work at the University and Museum Dawkins continued to give addresses and to publish a vast amount of research work of great value. Reference has been made to a few only but a few others might be mentioned. In 1901 he published a fine report on 'The Cairn and Sepulchral Cave at Gop, near Prestatyn'; in 1902, one on 'Bigbury Camp and the Pilgrims' Way', describing many iron objects found in the camp; in 1905, 'Pre-Roman Roads in North and East Yorkshire', also 'Permian and

Opening on 30th October 1912 of the new Egyptian Extension to the Manchester Museum. Right to left: Prof. W. Boyd Dawkins, Mr. N. L. Behrens, Prof. W. M. Flinders Petrie, Sir F. Forbes Adam, Sir Alfred Hopkinson, Mr. Jesse Howarth (standing), Mr. E. J. Broadfield, Prof. Elliot Smith, Sir W. H. Tattersall. Photo: Buxton Museum.

Carboniferous rocks in High Street, Manchester'; in 1909, 'Durham, York and Manchester in Prehistoric Times'. In 1910, he gave the Huxley Memorial Lecture at the Royal Anthropological Institute on 'The Arrival of Man in Britain in the Pleistocene Age', and spoke highly of Huxley and his great assistance in organising the old Manchester Museum and the geological department at Owens College. In 1912, he gave a Presidential Address to the Cambrian Archaeological Association on 'Certain fixed points in the Pre-History of Wales'. In that year he also figured and described a graptolite *(Monograptus priodon)* from the Silurian (Wenlock) strata obtained from the Chilham boring near Canterbury. In 1914, he gave a Presidential Address to the Cambrian Association on 'The Retreat of the Welsh from Wiltshire'. In 1921 he published an account of 'The Dwellers in Wiltshire in Prehistoric Times'. In 1922, he gave a Presidential Address to the Somerset Society on 'The Ethnology of Somerset from the Neolithic Age to the close of the Roman Dominion'. In 1924, he gave a Presidential Address to the Archaeological Institute on 'The Relation of the Prehistoric to the Pleistocene and Historic Periods'.

The excellent monograph on Wookey Hole (the Great Cave) by the late H. E. Balch, of Wells, Somerset, published in 1914, is dedicated to Boyd Dawkins, who wrote an exceedingly fine Preface of some twelve quarto pages. He emphasised the importance of Balch's work carried on under considerable difficulties, and reviewed the knowledge obtained from the caves of Somerset by many workers, and among other items, he made special mention of the two lake villages of Glastonbury and Meare discovered by Dr. A. Bulleid and worked by him and St. George Gray over many years. In connection with the latter, Dawkins arranged for me to go to Glastonbury to analyse and measure the large collection of animal remains found at the Lake Village during the excavations. I spent a week or more at the storeroom in 1914 carrying out this work, and in 1917 Dawkins and I published a joint account of these remains.

In 1918 Dawkins received the Prestwich Medal from the Geological Society of London. He already possessed the Lyell Medal, presented in 1889.

In June 1928 a most important addition was made to the City of Manchester Art Gallery by Sir William and Lady Boyd Dawkins. The gift consisted of pictures, furniture, Cloisonné enamels, and a collection illustrating the 'Dawn of Art'. The latter, made by Sir William, comprised copies of mural frescoes and engravings on cave walls in Southern France and North Spain. Other gifts were casts from original bones, antler and ivory, from French caves. These had been coloured by Sir William and Lady Dawkins, and, with the frescoes, represent the art of the Upper Palaeolithic cave-dwellers.

Dawkins was for 17 years a member of the Art Gallery Committee and put in a good deal of hard work. He was an enthusiastic supporter of the project for an art gallery on the Piccadilly site in Manchester after the removal of the Infirmary. He stressed the matter in an article in the Manchester Guardian of 9th March, 1903 and pointed out that the site offered an unrivalled opportunity of establishing in one central place the Free Library, enlarged Art Galleries, and a commercial museum to meet the needs of our ever-changing commerce.

In politics, Dawkins was a Unionist and held office in the Manchester Conservative and Unionist Association and in 1918 became the President of the Manchester University Constitutional Association. For some twenty-five years he was a Justice of the Peace.

Dawkins' advice on museum matters was eagerly sought after and willingly given. One of the last public services rendered by him was the opening of the new Buxton Museum in September 1928. This was not his first visit to the town as he brought parties of his geology students on several occasions and on one of these visits in 1886 he gave a lecture on Poole's Cavern at the Court House. He also visited the cavern and gave a talk there. In June 1893 he visited Buxton and gave lectures on the caves, the Carboniferous Limestone and associated sub-marine volcanoes. Later in the same month he paid another visit and lectured on the Millstone Grit and Coal Measures, also the springs. Soon after the discovery of Thirst House cave in Deep Dale he was again in the town when he

Interior of Sir William's home in Manchester at the turn of the century. The contents show some of Sir Williams' collecting interests, in particular in furniture (the Elizabethan cupboard was from New Hall, Castleton) and cloisonée enamels. Photo: Manchester Museum.

inspected the numerous Romano-British relics from the above cavern then housed in the 'lately formed' museum in the Town Hall, under the charge of T. A. Sarjent, the curator, and in the residence of Micah Salt in High Street. Dawkins also visited the cave and gave a talk. Dawkins' visit in September, 1928, was an event of great importance to Buxton as it was in order to open the new and enlarged library and museum in the Peak Buildings. Dawkins was then over 90 years of age. The ceremony took place before a concourse of notable people. The Mayor, Councillor J. J. F. Pugh, presided. In his opening address, extempore for forty minutes without referring to a single note, Sir William referred to cave exploration in Derbyshire, the Roman remains found by Micah Salt and others, the first-class material in the museum and its value to education, amongst other matters. The vote of thanks was ably proposed by Alderman Dr. Bemrose and was seconded by the author of this biography. Dawkins stressed the importance of looking to the Manchester Museum for advice and it was through his influence that I was appointed Honorary Consultant at Buxton Museum.

Dawkins died on 15th January, 1929, and on 30th October of that year his magnificent library of some 400 works of various kinds was presented to the town of Buxton by Lady Boyd Dawkins, according to the wishes of the late Sir William. The presentation took place at a special ceremony and the opening of the Boyd Dawkins Reference Room housing the books was by Sir Arthur Keith, F.R.S., M.D., etc., supported by Sir Arthur Evans, F.R.S., D.Litt., and Professor A. H. Sayce, D.Litt., etc. Councillor Pugh occupied the chair and was accompanied by Mrs. Pugh. Supporting them on the

Opening of the original Boyd Dawkins Room, 30th October, 1929. Right to left. Dr. J. W. Jackson, Sir Arthur Evans, Miss Twentyman, Lady Keith, Professor Sayce, Lady Boyd Dawkins, and Sir Arthur Keith. Dawkins married secondly Mary Congreave (1864-1954) the widow of the civil engineer Hubert Congreve who died in 1911. Photo: Buxton Museum.

platform were Lady Boyd Dawkins, Lady Keith, and many distinguished guests were in the audience.

In the above library the books are housed in three handsome bookcases of rose-wood, inlaid with ivory and brass, in the style of Louis Napoleon. Another feature in the room is a bronze bust of Sir William. Many photographs of great scientists and friends are on the walls along with a fine portrait of Darwin framed with a letter of the great scientist to Dawkins thanking him for his "magnificent" story of cave-hunting. The two medals, Lyell and Prestwich, were included in the gift. Some of the books include letters of the particular author, and on the margins of some books are detailed notes by Dawkins with comments such as "no" or "nonsense", "piffle", "rubbish" or even "tosh".

Editor's Note

The 'new' Boyd Dawkins Room contains all of the above mentioned items, and also additional material associated with Dawkins. On acquiring the J. W. Jackson Collection it became evident that Sir William had passed on to Jackson many books, offprints, manuscripts and correspondence, including such important items as Dawkins's own copies of the British Pleistocene Mammalia Monographs. The Dawkins archive and library is now more complete than ever since his death.

The British Association meeting at Leeds, 1927. Left to right: Dr. M. Foster, Sir W. Boyd Dawkins, Dr. G. R. Bidder, Lt.Col. Kitson Clark, Dr. E. J. Allan, Prof. E. W. MacBride. Photo: Buxton Museum.

BIBLIOGRAPHY

[This list of Dawkins' principal publications is a much expanded version of Dr. Jackson's 'Selected Bibliography', but like his listing is still by no means complete — Ed.]

1862 Traces of the Early Britons in the Neighbourhood of Oxford. *Oxford Archit. & Hist. Soc. Report,* 8pp

1862-3 On a Hyaena Den at Wookey Hole, near Wells. *Q.J.G.S.,* XVIII, p.115-125, XIX, p.260-274

1863 On a Romano-British Cemetery, and a Roman Camp at Hordham, in West Sussex. *Sussex Archaeol. Coll.,* XVI, 15pp

1863 On the Dentition of *Rhinoceros tichorhinus. Nat. Hist. Rev.* No. XII, p.525-38

1864 On the Rhaetic Beds and White Lias of Somerset. *Q.J.G.S.,* XX, p.396-412

1864 On the Caverns of Burrington Combe. *Proc. Som. Arch. & Nat. Hist. Soc.,* XII, Pt.2, 16pp

1865 Note on the Palaeontology of the Rhaetic Beds in Western and Central Somerset. *Geol. Mag.,* II, p.481-484

1865 On the Dentition of *Rhinoceros megarhinus. Nat. Hist. Rev.,* V, 16pp

1865 On the Dentition of *Hyaena spelaea. Ibid.,* V, p.80-96

1865 On the Mammalian Remains found by E. Wood near Richmond, Yorks. *Q.J.G.S.,* Nov. p.493-5

1866 On the Dentition of *Rhinoceros leptorhinus,* Owen. *Proc. Roy. Soc.,* XV, p.106

1866 The Habits and Conditions of the Two Earliest Known Races of Men. *Q.J. of Sci.* 1866

1866 On the Pleistocene Mammals of Yorkshire (Abstract). *Leeds Phil. Trans.,* 9pp

1866 On the Pleistocene Mammals of Yorkshire. *Proc. Geol. Polytech. Soc. of W.R. Yorks.* Aug. 6th 1866. 11pp

1866 Eskimos in the South of Gaul. *Saturday Review.,* Dec. 8

1866-7 On British Fossil Oxen. *Q.J.G.S.,* 22, p.391-401, 23, p.176-184

1866-72 The British Pleistocene Mammalia. *Pal. Soc.,* Pts.I-IV

1867 Brother Prince. *Macmillan's Mag.,* Oct., p.464-473

1867 On the Age of the Lower Brick Earths of the Thames Valley. *Q.J.G.S.* XXIII, p.91-109

1867 On the Dentition of *Rhinoceros leptorhinus* Owen. *Ibid.,* p.213-228

1867 *Ovibos moschatus. Proc. Roy. Soc.,* XV, p.516

1867-8 Sur les Mammifères pleistocenes que l'on a trouvés associés à l'homme dans la Grande-Bretagne. Internat. Congress of Prehistoric Archaeology. Transln. *Intellect. Observer* Oct., p.201-206, Jan., p.403-410

1867 On the Pre-Historic Mammalia found Associated with Man in Great Britain. Lecture given at the opening of the Blackmore Museum, Salisbury

1868 Early Antiquities in Portugal. *Trans. Int. Congr. Preh. Archaeol.,* 3rd Session, 7pp

1868 The Progress of Civilisation in Northern and Western Europe in Prehistoric Times. *Fraser's Mag.* June, p.776-782

1868 The Variation of animals and plants under domestication. *Edinb. Rev.,* Oct., p. 414-450

1868 On a new species of Fossil Deer from Clacton. *Q.J.G.S.,* XXIV, p.511-518

1868 On a new species of Fossil Deer from the Norwich Crag. *Ibid.,* p.516-8

1868 On the Dentition of *Rhinoceros etruscus,* Falc. *Ibid.,* p.207-218

1868 The Former Range of the Reindeer in Europe. *Pop. Sc. Rev.,* p.34-45

1868 The Former Range of the Mammoth in Europe. *Ibid.,* p.275-286

1868 Dr. Falconer and his labours in India. *J. Travel and Nat. Hist.,* p.800-816

1868 On the Value of the Evidence for the Existence of the Mammoth in Europe in Pre-Glacial Times. *Geol. Mag.,* V, No. 7, 6pp

1868 The Iron mines of the Weald. *Trans. Internat. Cong. Prehist. Arch.* 6pp

1868 On the Prehistoric Mammalia of Great Britain. *Ibid.,* 22pp

1868 On the Discovery of Flint and Chert under a Submerged Forest. *Ibid.*

1869 On the Distribution of the British Postglacial Mammals. *Q.J.G.S.,* XXV, p.192-217

1869 The British Lion. *Pop. Sc. Rev.,* No. 31, p.150-158

1869 Pleistocene Fauna, Kents Hole. *Rept. Brit. Assoc.*

1869 Discoveries in Turquoise Mines in Sinatic Promontory. *Mem. & Proc. Mach. Lit. & Phil. Soc.,* Dec. 14th, p.43

1870 Geological Theory in Britain. *Edinb. Rev.,* Jan., p.39-64

1870 Prehistoric Times. *Ibid.,* Sept., p.439-479

1870 On Coal, Science Lectures for the People. Second Series. 16pp. *Manchester*

1870 The Geological Calculus. *Nature,* March, p.505-6

1870 Fossil Mammals in North America. *Ibid.,* June, p.119-20, July, p.232-3

1870 On the Discovery of Flint and Chert under a Submerged Forest in W. Somerset. *Journ. Ethn. Soc.,* II, p.141-5

1870 Primitive Man. *Nature,* Aug., p.311-2

1870 The Denbighshire Caves. *Trans. Manch. Geol. Soc.,* IX, p.31-7

1870-1 Cave Hunting. *Macmillan's Mag.,* Oct., p.452-60., Nov., p.105-113, Sept., p.357-366

1871 Darwin on the Descent of Man. *Edinb. Rev.,* July, p.195-235

1871 On the Discovery of the Glutton in Britain. *Q.J.G.S.,* XXVI, 4pp

1871 British Bears and Wolves. *Pop. Sc. Rev.,* p.241-253

1871 On the Discovery of Platyenemic Men in Denbighshire. *Journ. Ethnol Soc.,* II, p.440-450

1871 Report on the Victoria Cave, Settle. *Journ. Anthrop. Inst.,* I, p.60-70

1871 The Geology of Oxford. *Nature.* Dec., p.145-148

1871 On the Formation of the Caves around Ingleborough. *Trans. Manch. Geol. Soc.,* X, p.106-112

1872 The Climate of the Pleistocene Age. *Ibid.,* XI, p.45-52

1872 The Present Phase of Prehistoric Archaeology. *British Quarterly,* Oct., p.443-487

1872 Crystals of Calcite and Iron Sulphide Surrounding Bitumen from Castleton. *Mem. & Proc. Manch. Lit. & Phil. Soc.,* XI, No. 9, p.94. Also *Pop. Sci. Rev.,* XI, p.204

1872 On the Classification of the Pleistocene Strata in Britain and the Continent by means of the Mammalia. *Q.J.G.S.,* XXVIII, p.410-446

1872 On the Cervidae of the Forest Bed of Norfolk and Suffolk. *Ibid.,* p.405-410

1872 Pleistocene Climate and Mammals. *Pop. Sc. Rev.*

1872 Report on the Victoria Cave, Settle. *Brit. Assn. Rept.*

1872 On the Physical Geography of the Mediterranean. *Ibid.*

1872 *(Musk Ox.) Brit. Pleist, Mam. Pt.5, I, pts.I-V (See 1867 Pal. Soc.)*

1872 Ancient Geography of the West of England. *Som. Arch. & N. Hist. Soc.,* Sept. 10, 6pp

1873 Observations on the Rate at which Stalagmite is being accumulated in the Ingleborough Cave. *Rept. Brit. Assn.,* 80. Also *Mem. & Proc. Manch. Lit. & Phil. Soc.,* April

1873 The Results of the Settle Cave Exploration. *Mem. & Proc. Manch. Lit. & Phil. Soc.,* XII, No. 7, p.61-5

1874 The Northern Range of the Basques. *Mem. & Proc. Manch. Lit. & Phil. Soc.,* XIII, p. 81-89, and in *Fornightly Rev.,* XVI, p.322-337

1874 On the Northern Range of the Fallow Deer in Europe. *Nature,* Dec., p.112-114

1874 Antiquity of Man. *British Quarterly.* April

1874 Cave Hunting. Macmillan & Co. London

1874 The Limits of our Knowledge of the Earth. In Essays and Addresses by Professors and Lecturers at the Owens College, Manchester, p.113-133

1874 Discovery of Grooved Stone Hammers at Alderley Edge Copper Mines. *Journ. Anthrop. Inst. G.B. & I.,* V, and *Manch. Lit. & Phil. Soc.,* XIV

1875 The Mammalia found at Windy Knoll, Derbyshire, *Q.J.G.S.,* XXXI, p.246-255

1875 On the Stone Mining Tools from Alderley Edge, Cheshire. *J. Anthrop Inst.,* V, p.2-5

1875 Geikie's Life of Murchison. *Edinb. Rev.,* July, p.173-203

1876 On the water supply in the Red Rocks of Lancashire and Cheshire. Inaugural Address. *Trans. Manch. Geol. Soc.,* 11pp

1876 Bancroft's Native Races of North America. *Edinb. Rev.*, Oct., p.283-318

1876 On the Mammalia and Traces of Man found in the Robin Hood Cave. *Q.J.G.S.* XXXII, p.245-258

1877 On the Ossiferous Deposit at Windy Knoll, Castleton, Derbyshire. *Ibid.,* p.724-729

1877 The Organisation of Natural History Museums. *Nature,* June, p.137-8

1877 The Antiquity of Man. *Ibid.,* June, p.97-8

1877 On the Mammal-Fauna of the Caves of Cresswell Crags. *Q.J.G.S.,* XXXIII, p.589-612

1877 On the Evidence afforded by the Caves of Great Britain as to the Antiquity of Man. *Journ. Anthrop. Inst.,* VII, p.151-162, 174-185

1878 On the Deer of the European Miocene and Pliocene Strata, *Q.J.G.S.,* XXXIV, p.402-420. See also *Q.J.G.S.,* XXXIX, (1883), p.579

1879 Our Earliest Ancestors in Britain. Sci. Lectures for the People No. 6. Tenth Series. Manchester, p.95-106

1879 With J. M. MELLO. Further Discoveries in the Cresswell Caves. *Q.J.G.S.,* XXXV, p.724-735

1879 On the Range of the Mammoth in Space and Time. *Ibid.,* pl.138-147

1880 Early Man in Britain. Macmillan & Co., London

1880 The Classification of the Tertiary Period by means of the Mammalia. *Q.J.G.S.,* XXXVI, p.379-405

1882 On the Range of *Anodonta jukesii. Trans Manch. Geol. Soc.,* XVI, 4pp

1882 The Channel Tunnel. *Ibid.,* 20pp

1882 The Ancient Ethnology of Wales. *Y Cymmrodor,* V, pt.2, 15pp

1883 Early Man in America. *North Am. Rev.,* 137, p.338-349

1883 The "Silver Streak" and the Channel Tunnel. *Contemp. Rev.,* Feb., p.240-249

1883 Memorandum on the Proposed Channel Tunnel, based mainly on the Blue Books — C.1206 and C.3358, presented to the Houses of Parliament, 11pp

1883 On the Alleged Existence of *Ovibos moschatus* in the Forest Bed and its Range in space and time. *Q.J.G.S.,* XXXIX, p.575-581

1883 The English Conquest of Britain. *Trans. Lancs. & Cheshire Antiq. Soc.,* I, (1884 for 1883), p.105

1884 Lancashire and Cheshire in Prehistoric Times. (Pres. Addr.) *Ibid.,* II, (1885 for 1884), 7pp

1885 Canada and the Great North West. *Trans. Manch. Geol. Soc.,* 16pp

1885 On a Hoard of Articles found at Heaton, near Norwich. *Proc. Soc. Antiq.,* XI, 10pp

1885 On some deposits of Apatite near Ottawa, Canada. *Trans. Manch. Geol. Soc.,* 9pp

1885 On a skull of *Ovibos moschatus* from the sea-bottom. *Q.J.G.S.,* XLI, p.242-244

1886 On the Geography of Britain in the Carboniferous Period. *Trans. Manch. Geol. Soc.,* Nov. 9, 11pp

1887 The Discovery of Britain. *Trans. Manch. Geogr. Soc.,* Feb., 25pp

1887 Memorandum on the Present aspect of the Channel Tunnel Question, presented to the Houses of Parliament, 6pp

1887 The Ornamentation of the Early Irish MSS and of the Runic Crosses. *The Manx Note Book,* July, 5pp

1888 On the Geography of Britain in the Carboniferous Period. *Trans. Manch. Geol. Soc.,* XIX, p.37-47

1888 On *Ailurus anglicus,* a new carnivore from the Red Crag. (Norfolk and Suffolk) *Q.J.G.S.,* XLIV, p.228-231

1889 The Place of the Welsh in the History of Britain. Reprinted from the *Manchester Examiner.* London & Manchester, 48pp

1890 On the clay Slates and Phyllites of the South of the Isle of Man. *Trans. Manch. Geol. Soc.,* XX, p.53-7

1890 The Discovery of Coal Measures near Dover. *Ibid.,* p.502-12

1890 The Search for Coal in the South of England. *Royal Inst. G.B.,* June, 9pp

1891 The Channel Tunnel. *J. Manch. Geog. Soc.,* VII, p.81-83

1892 The Further Discovery of Coal at Dover and its bearing on the Coal Question. *Trans. Manch. Geol. Soc.,* XXI, p.456-474

1893 The Place of the Lake Dwellings at Glastonbury in British Archaeology. *Natural Science,* III, No.21, p.344-6

1893 Report on Supplemental Supply from Wells in the London Area. Statement in evidence before the Royal Commission on the Metropolitan Water Supply. Appendix C44, p.419

1893 Geology in Relation to Geography. *J. Manch. Geog. Soc.,* Feb., 5pp

1894 On the Relation of the Palaeolithic to the Neolithic period. *J. Anthrop. Inst.,* XXII, p.242-254

1894 Preface in M. GORDON, Life and Correspondence of William Buckland, London

1894 The Coalfields of New South Wales. *Trans. Manch. Geol. Soc.,* XXII, p.160-9

1894 William Pengelly. Obituary Notice. *Proc. Roy. Soc.,* 59, p.xxxix-xli

1894 The Probable Range of the Coal-Measures in Southern England. *Trans. Inst. Mining Engin.,* VIII, 13pp

1894 On the South-Eastern Coalfield at Dover. *Trans. Manch. Geol. Soc.,* XXII, p.488-505

1894-5 On the Geology of the Isle of Man. *Ibid.,* p.590-606, *Ibid.,* XXIII, p.147-158

1895 Opening Address of the Antiquarian Section at the Scarborough Meeting. *Archaeol. Journ.* Dec., p.336-347

1896 Bosnia-Herzegovina and Dalmatia. *Nature,* Jan.

1897 The Present Phase of Prehistoric Archaeology. *Archaeol. Journ.* Dec., 18pp

1898 On the History of the Discovery of the S. Eastern Coalfield. *Trans. Manch. Geol. Soc.,* XXV, p.155-60

1898 On the Relation of Geology to Engineering. *Proc. Inst. Civil Engin.,* CXXXIV, 26pp

1898 Hod Hill. *Proc. Dorset Nat. Hist. and Antiq. Field Club,* XIX, p.LXXX-V

1899 The Chartley White Cattle. *N. Staffs. F.C.,* Jan., 7pp

1899 On the South-Eastern Coal-Field. *Geol. Mag.,* VI, p.501-5

1900 Early Man in Hampshire. Victoria County History

1900 The Exploration of Hod Hill, near Blandford Dorset. *Archaeol. Journ.* March, 17pp

1901 Skulls from Cave Burials. *Ann. Report. British School at Athens,* No. vii, p.150-5

1901 On the Cairn and Sepulchral Cave at Gop, near Prestatyn. *Archaeol. Journ.,* LVIII, No. 231, 322-341

1901 The Influence of the Mediterranean Peoples in Prehistoric Britain. *Nature,* 65, p.39-40

1901 The Exploration of Prehistoric Sepulchral Remains of the Bronze Age at Bleasdale by S. Jackson. *Trans. Lancs. & Cheshire Antiq. Soc.,* XVIII, 12pp

1902 Remains of Man found in the Dictaean Cave in 1901. *Man.,* p.114

1902 A Sketch of the Physiography and Geology of Manchester. Handbook and Guide to Manchester, British Assoc.

1902 The Red Sandstone-Rocks of Peel. *Q.J.G.S.,* LVIII, p.633-646

1902 The Carboniferous, Permian, and Triassic Rocks under the Glacial Drift in the North of the Isle of Man. *Ibid.,* p.647-660

1902 On Bigbury Camp and the Pilgrims Way. *Archaeol. Journ.,* LIX, p.211-218. (Repr. as Manch. Mus. Handbook No. 12, 1903)

1903 Prehistoric Art and Archaeology — Maycenaen Art. *Trans. Lancs. & Cheshire Antiq. Soc.,* XX, 6pp

1903 The Buried Coal-Fields of Southern England. Statement in Evidence before the Royal Commission on Coal Supply. Final Report, part x, p.26-35

1903 Ossiferous Fissure at Dove Holes, near Buxton. *Q.J.G.S.,* LIX, p.105-129

1903 The Opportunity of Manchester: The Infirmary Site. Reprinted from *Manch. Guardian* of 9th March, 1903

1904 On the Pre-Roman Roads of Northern and Eastern Yorkshire. *Archaeol. Journ.,* LXI, p.309-318

1904 On the Discovery of Elephas antiquus at Blackpool. *Mem. & Proc. Manch. Lit. & Phil. Soc.,* XLVIII, 4pp

1904 The Permian and Carboniferous Rocks in a Section in High Street, Chorlton-on-Medlock, Manchester. *Trans. Manch. Geol. Soc.,* XXIX, p.37-40 and *Trans. Inst. Mining Engin.* 1905

1904 A Section of the Glacial Deposits met with the construction of the New Dock at Salford. *Ibid.,* p.34-6 and *Trans. Inst. Mining Eng.*

1905 The Ancient Roads Connected with Melandra and the Site. *Rept. Manch. and Dist. Branch of the Classical Assn.*

1906 The Origin of the Welsh People. *Welsh Review,* I, No. 1, p.1-3

1906 Early Man in Somerset. Victoria County History

1907 The Discovery of the South-Eastern Coal-Field. *J. Soc. Arts.,* LV, p.450-8

1907 Tre'r Ceiri. *Archaeol. Cambrensis,* Jan., p.35-7

1909 Notes on Durham, York and Manchester — Prehistoric Times. *Arch. Journ.,* LXVI, p.171-4

1910 The arrival of Man in Britain in the Pleistocene Age. (Huxley Memorial Lecture). *Journ. Roy. Anthrop. Inst.,* XL, July-Dec.

1912 The Ancient Sources of the Endowments of the Church of England. Sherratt & Hughes, London, 14pp

1912 On some points in the Prehistoric Archaeology of Somerset. (Pres. Address). *Proc. Som. Arch. & Nat. Hist. Soc.,* LVIII, p.13-25

1912 Certain Fixed Points in the Prehistory of Wales. (Pres. Address). *Arch. Camb.,* Jan., p.61-108

1912 A Graptolite *(Monograptus priodon)* from the Silurian (Wenlock) Strata from the Chilham Boring Near Caterbury. *Trans. Manch. Geol. Soc.,* 33, p.49

1913 The S. Eastern Coal-field, the Associated Rocks and the Buried Plateau. *Trans. Inst. Mining Engin.,* XLIV, p.350-378

1913 The Settlement of Britain in the Prehistoric Age. In Essays & Studies presented to William Ridgeway. C.U.P. 1913, p.427-435

1914 The Retreat of the Welsh from Wiltshire. (Pres. Address). *Arch. Camb.,* Vol. XIV, 28pp

1915 The Classification of the Tertiary Strata by means of the Eutherian Mammals. Rept. Brit. Assn. Manch. Sect. C

1916 The Antiquity of Man and Dawn of Art in Europe. *Edin. Rev.,* July, p.80-98

1917 (Human Remains) in *The Glastonbury Lake Village* by Bulleid and Gray, 1917, Vol. ii, 673-684

1918 The Organisation of Museums and Art Galleries in Manchester. *Mem. & Proc. Manch. Lit. & Phil. Soc.,* 62, 11pp

1918 On a find of Neolithic Celts near Crickhowell, Breconshire. *Arch. Camb.,* XVIII, 5pp

1920 The Geography of Britain at the time of the arrival of Man. *J. Manch. Geog. Soc.,* XXXVI, p.1-6

1921 The Dwellers in Wiltshire in Prehistoric Times. *Arch. Journ.,* LXXVIII, p.309-12 and 2nd Series XXVIII, p.251-263

1922 The Ethnology of Somerset from the Neolithic Age to the close of the Roman Dominion. (Pres. Address). *Proc. Som. Arch. & Nat. Hist. Soc.,* LXVIII, p.1-7

1928 Pictures, Furniture, Enamels and a Collection Illustrating the Dawn of Art (pres. to Manch. City Art Gallery). Handbook, p.1-31

1928 The Manchester Museum: Its Place in Education. *Old Owensian Journal,* V, No. 4, June

1929 The Relation of the Prehistoric to the Pleistocene and the Historic Periods. *Arch. Journ.,* LXXXI, p.321-41 and second series Vol. XXXI, p.1-20. (Pres. Address to inst. 1924). reprint of 1924

DR. J. WILFRID JACKSON (1880-1978)

A Biographical Sketch

by Michael J. Bishop

JOHN WILFRID JACKSON was born at Scarborough on the 15th June, 1880 the second of six children of Thomas and Mary Jackson of York. His parents had married in 1877, and seeking employment his father Thomas Jackson moved in 1878 to Manchester, the rest of the family finally joining him in the winter of 1881/2. J. W. Jackson lived in Manchester from this time on until 1945 when he moved to Buxton, Derbyshire.

Dr. Jackson's parents, Thomas Jackson (1853-1912) and Mary Jackson (1855-1936 née Bosomworth) who married in 1877.
Photo: Miss A. S. Jackson

Little is recorded of his early childhood and school days in Manchester, though later in life he recalled a visit made with his parents in 1887 to the Royal Jubilee Exhibition in Manchester and another in the same year to Buffalo Bill's Wild West Show in Salford! He thought that his interest in geology and conchology might well have been seeded by visits when very young to the Scarborough seashore.

In about 1892 he entered his first job as an office boy on the staff of the 'Clarion' newspaper, and by the following year had joined the cotton spinners, Ashworth & Silkstone as an assistant with whom he remained about two years. During this period (1894) Jackson recalled being taken to see the procession in which Queen Victoria opened the Manchester Ship Canal, and remembered it was a period during which he helped his father on a part time basis with his accounts and at times in his smithy. His first long term employment came in about 1895/6 when he joined the large South American shipping firm Kolp, Kullman & Co., with whom he held several positions finally becoming Assistant Woollen Buyer (1904-1907). This was an important time for Jackson, for apart from going through ordinary business training he was also encouraged to attend classes in languages at the Lower Mosley Street Schools (1902-4) and having received certificates in shorthand, English, Spanish and Latin, he followed these up in 1906 by entering classes in Geology at the Municipal School of Technology (now U.M.I.S.T.) he left Kolp, Kullman & Co. in 1907 to join the Manchester Museum.

Jackson, as has been intimated, took up his interest in science during his employment with Kolp's. Jackson himself recalled that the pursuit of his first love in science, conchology, dated back to Mafeking Night, 12th May 1900, when he was invited to visit the home of Robert Standen to inspect his shell collection. Robert Standen (1854-1925) was a naturalist born and bred in Lancashire, who held for most of his career the post of

Robert Standen, the conchologist, (1854-1925), and his daughter Alicia Mayor Standen whom Jackson married in 1906, at their Manchester home in 1905. Photo: Miss A. S. Jackson.

Assistant Keeper in the Zoological Department of the Manchester Museum, and whose speciality throughout his life was the study of the mollusca.

The results of their meeting in 1900 were far reaching, for Jackson had by December 1900 been nominated a member of the Conchological Society, and was duly elected a member in January 1901. Standen introduced Jackson to many well known conchologists such as R. D. Darbyshire and J. Cosmo Melvill, and on a more personal basis Jackson met his daughter Alicia whom he married in 1906, establishing a lifelong link with the Standen family which he much valued.

Fired with enthusiasm for natural history, Jackson in the years before his appointment to the Manchester Museum pursued energetically conchology, geology, and botany whenever the time and opportunity availed. In 1901 he started investigating the geology and conchology of Castleton, Miller's Dale, Buxton, and Matlock, and in the same year his first conchological paper, on the mollusca of Castleton was read to the Conchological Society, while his first geological paper, on the shell marls of Silverdale appeared in 1905.

We know a great deal of his activities during 1904 as he for the only time in his life kept a full daily diary of his activities. From this source his devotion to conchology is most striking, and the interest and expertise he built up in these formative years was to last for the rest of his long life. Jackson had collected molluscs extensively in the Silverdale district, and as with most naturalists of his day was active in exchanging specimens. He was at the same time attending Conchological Society meetings, exhibiting his collection at special meetings, and was engaged in attending and leading field trips (n.b. with the Conchological Society and the newly formed Lower Mosley Street Natural History Society). Jackson in July of 1904 took advantage of his holidays to visit Ireland for the first time. He had corresponded and exchanged shells with Robert Welch, a naturalist and photographer of some standing in Ireland, who like Jackson had not only been introduced to the Conchological Society by Robert Standen but was later in life President of the Society, and upon his visit to Belfast made immediate contact with him. Jackson's other main destination on this trip was to visit the Larne Biological station and the naturalist Joseph Peason with whom he spent many days collecting specimens and assisted at the Station's laboratories in examining fish. During this first Irish trip Robert Standen's wife, the mother of Jackson's future wife, died.

In September of 1904 Jackson had been elected into the Council of the Conchological Society, and following the Irish trip and his many collecting rambles earlier in the year spent the rest of 1904 busily studying and writing up the results of his collecting. In November 1904 he undertook his first term as a 'curator' of collections other than his own, when he offered to rearrange the Museum of St. Bede's College, Salford, which had become very neglected.

Robert Welch's influence on Jackson is evident in the interest that Jackson took up in photography. Following his Irish visit Welch frequently sent Jackson photographs of natural history specimens, and Jackson reciprocated in having photos taken and began developing prints himself. In December 1904 Jackson records buying his first plate camera, and for the rest of his life photographed, developed and printed all his own material.

In taking up his serious interest in natural history at this time, he made his first contacts by correspondence with a number of important scientists such as W. B. Wright, McKenny Hughes and A. S. Kennard with whom he became a close colleague later in life. Although conchology was clearly his primary interest in the first decade of this century, geology clearly ran a close second, and the subject was important enough for him to attend classes between 1906 and 1909. It is likely that Sir William Boyd Dawkins may have been partly responsible for this shift in interest, since Jackson attended his public lectures on geology and archaeology prior to 1907.

Of the many of his conchological papers

J. Wilfrid Jackson, Robert Standen and Alicia Standen at Windy Knoll Cave, Castleton, about 1905. Photo: Buxton Museum, taken by the naturalist and photographer Robert Welch (1859-1936).

and notes in scientific journals before 1910, one of the most substantial was his bibliography of the non-marine mollusca of Lancashire published 1907-8, Tackling this sort of subject shows how well Jackson had grasped taxonomic and bibliographical practise at such an early stage in his career.

The year 1907 marked a turning point in his life, for in June of that year he was appointed Assistant Keeper of the Manchester Museum under Dr. W. E. Hoyle. Sir William Boyd Dawkins was on the interview panel for this post, and in Jackson's words gave him a 'rigorous interview'. On taking up his post in the Museum Dawkins supervised Jackson in his curatorial duties and also supervised him in research upon the osteology of mammals. Jackson thus followed Dawkins in this specialist study and became an authority on identifying bone remains, to whom many archaeologists turned later in his career for specialist reports. Jackson adapted to the Museum extremely quickly — remarkably in view of his previous employment as a woollen buyer, but perhaps understandably in that he had after all moved in on a full time basis to a way of life that had previously been his hobby. Barely within a fortnight of taking up his post he delivered his first museum lecture on the formation of China Clay! Another immediate result of his Museum appointment was that he began visiting various geological localities for the Museum — in September 1907 he was collecting geological specimens from Kirkby Lonsdale and Hutton Roof quarries — and he came into direct contact with various departments within the Museum which played a very important part in broadening his horizons and interests. We find for instance that he was assisting in cataloguing the Egyptian collections in 1907 and 1908, and on 6th May, 1908 assisted Margaret Murray in the famous mummy unrolling in front of a Manchester audience (see photo).

The year 1907 was also an important year in the field since Jackson started investigating Dog Holes, Warton Crag, which occupied much of his time to 1913 and was his first serious study of pleistocene remains from caves. Jackson's first caving paper came out in 1909 as a result of his

Mummy-unrolling before an audience at Manchester University, 6th May, 1908. Left to right: Robert Standen, Miss Wilkinson, Margaret Murray, and J. W. Jackson. Photo: Buxton Museum.

investigations at Dog Holes and was followed up by a whole series of further reports. Jackson made personal contact with Professor McKenny Hughes in 1909 who visited him while excavating at Dog Holes in 1909.

Jackson's output of papers testifies well to his activities up to the First World War, when over and above his conchological and mammalian papers we see him publishing in other areas of palaentology mainly as a result of his Museum work, and importantly in 1912 on recent Brachiopoda from the Scottish National Antarctic Expedition, a field he maintained a special interest in all his life.

Before the outbreak of war, Jackson joined the Manchester Volunteer Defence Corps, and during the war served as a Special Constable with the Manchester City Police in which as a member of the Ambulance Corps he received in 1915 his Ambulance Certificate of the Order of St. John. He was also a member of the Manchester University Officers Training Corps.

Before the war Jackson had received a grant from the Royal Society of London to undertake geological survey work in the Dovedale area, and this work he managed to continue intermittently through the war years, and he took it up again with vigour after the war. Other work in the war years was mainly tied up with his conchological studies, most significant of all being the publication in 1917 of his book 'Shells as Evidence of the Migrations of Early Culture' which brought together a number of papers that he had read to the Manchester Literary and Philosophical Society. This work had been prompted by Grafton Elliot Smith who had been studying various aspects of 'The Migrations of Early Culture', as his own book was entitled.

Elliot Smith was interested in any areas of archaeology and ethnography that might support his diffusionist theories, and upon learning something of the cultural uses of shells in various corners of the world, approached Jackson to investigate the subject from a scientific and ethnographical point of view. Although Elliot Smith's extreme views have been largely abandoned, Jackson's book remains a highly interesting accumulation of facts on the subject of shells in prehistoric and primitive societies. Jackson's devotion to conchology was marked by another event in 1917, for he was elected Secretary of the Conchological Society of Great Britain in that year, a position he maintained until retiring in 1945.

Jackson did much work on recent and fossil brachiopods before the 1920's, notably working on another series of specimens from one of the Antarctic Expeditions, this time the Terra Nova Expedition, the results of which were published by the British Museum (Natural History) in 1918. His specialist knowledge of recent brachiopods was drawn upon in later years too when he worked upon specimens from the Siboga and Mortensen expeditions.

J. Wilfrid Jackson and his wife Alicia Mayor Jackson during the First World War, when he joined up in the Special Police Reserve.

The war years saw a rather special professional relationship with Sir William Boyd Dawkins, for both men contributed important sections to Bulleid and Gray's second volume of the Glastonbury Lake Village excavations, published in 1917.

Dawkins' main contribution to Bulleid and Gray was on various aspects of the human remains discovered, while Jackson essentially did all the work on the animal remains. This initial contact with Bulleid developed into a long friendship, and he and Jackson were to produce further valuable joint work twenty years on.

Jackson's activities in the inter-war years can roughly be divided into two main decades, 1918 to 1928, when his most important output was in the field of geology, and 1928-1938 when his main output was in producing bone reports for various archaeological excavations. In both cases the two world wars mark changes in his activities and output, after the First War he spent far less time with conchology in favour of geology and archaeology, while the end of the Second War coincided with his retirement from the Manchester Museum, following which his work and pursuits were very broadly based.

In the first inter-war decade, 1918 to 1928, Jackson continued his detailed study of the geology of the Dovedale area, and was active in studying various areas of North Derbyshire geology and palaeontology, especially of the Edale area. The late twenties were a particularly important period in this geological work since the Geological Survey of Great Britain were active in the North Derbyshire and Manchester areas at this time and Jackson came into close contact with many of their officers, in particular W. B. Wright, supplying important field observations, identifications of fossils collected from these areas, and of course giving them access to the Manchester Museum collections. A particularly valuable piece of work undertaken by Jackson, was the study of the geological succession below the Kinder Scout Grit in North Derbyshire, in which he demonstrated the presence of the Namurian Zones by their content of fossil Goniatites. This work appeared as a number of papers in the 1920's and has been widely acknowledged by later workers as a most important contribution to Carboniferous stratigraphy.

Again Dr. Jackson's Dovedale work was important, particularly so when in 1930 he submitted evidence before the National Parks Commission on the geological importance of Dovedale, a contribution which has helped preserve this most important and picturesque area. Jackson built up during his studies of the Dovedale, Edale, and Castleton areas a highly important collection of many thousand Carboniferous fossils which are in Buxton Museum and serve as a highly valuable reference collection for any geologist studying the Peak District.

The subject of conchology was by no means forgotten in the twenties, and indeed Jackson published in 1925 one of his most significant papers in conchology, on the distribution of the Pearl Mussel in the British Isles. In 1927 he published a paper on the history of the Conchological Society of Great Britain.

Jackson's work was recognized by the University of Manchester in the 1920's, when the University conferred upon him the degree of Master of Science in 1921, and in 1929 the degree of Doctor of Science for his researches into geology, zoology, ethnography and prehistoric archaeology.

Dr. J. Wilfrid Jackson on being conferred Doctor of Science by Manchester University in 1929. Photo. Buxton Museum.

The twenties also saw him in active roles in many societies, in some of which he held office — notably as the first Honorary Secretary to the newly formed Manchester Geological Association in 1925 and President in 1927 (and again subsequently in 1955 and 1960), and he was elected President of the Conchological Society of Great Britain in 1923 (he was Secretary both sides of his Presidency). Another body he made special contact with was the W.E.A. in 1925, and for many years onward he ran geology classes and excursions with various branch groups. Of his contact with other Societies in the 20's, he was elected to the Geologists' Association in 1924, and the Yorkshire Geological Society in 1927.

A sad personal blow to Jackson and his family occurred in 1925 upon the death of his wife's father Robert Standen, with whom Jackson had such a close professional as well as personal relationship. His obituary notice of Standen is a touching tribute to his conscientious work and warm character. Following his death Jackson was promoted to Senior Assistant Keeper in succession to Standen and he held this office until his retirement from the Manchester Museum. Jackson records meeting in the Museum a fascinating spectrum of personalities, particularly between 1925 and 1928 when for instance he met as diverse a group of people as l'Abbé Breuil, Sir W. Flinders Petrie, King Fuad of Egypt and Sequah, Chief Red Beaver! Under the Museum Jackson also had the opportunity to do much travelling, and as a delegate of the University attended most of the British Association meetings in the 1920's, and in 1925 travelled abroad for the first time for a fortnight's congress and tour in and around Prague.

In 1923 the Duke of Portland granted the Derbyshire Cave Exploration Committee permission to conduct further excavations at Cresswell Crags. Sir William Boyd Dawkins was chairman of the Committee, A. Leslie Armstrong led the excavations, and Dr. Jackson became a member of the committee and was responsible for identifying the bones recovered. Armstrong started work in Pin Hole, taking over effectively where Mello and Dawkins had finished in the 1870's, and his excavations of Pin Hole and Mother Grundy's Parlour

Pin Hole Cave, Creswell Crags, 31st October, 1925. Right to left: J. W. Jackson, F. A. Holmes (kneeling), E. K. Tratman, L. S. Palmer, J. W. Puttrell, and 2 others. Photo: Buxton Museum, taken by A. I. Armstrong.

spanned 1924 to 1936, during which time Jackson was particularly active in 1925-27 and 1934. Armstrong did not live to complete this work on Cresswell, and much work fell to Jackson in collecting together his data and finds. The bulk of the remains from Pin Hole were housed in the Manchester Museum (over 11,000 specimens) and although the classification of the animal remains presented Jackson with no problems, it proved difficult to correlate the poorly marked data on the specimens with the excavated sections. One of Jackson's special contributions in reporting on the animal remains was his study of the rodent remains which have become such an important part today of the study of any pleistocene or more recent site. In Dawkins' day rodent remains were not considered of any importance, but the first quarter of the twentieth century saw their study advance enormously. Another special contribution of Jackson's at Cresswell, was his reporting of the mollusca from the cave, which he noted were usually ignored by cave explorers. Jackson was eminently qualified to report on both the non-marine and marine mollusca (brought in by man), and it was his wide knowledge of such specialist topics that really placed him as Britain's leading cave prehistorian from the 1920's to 1960's.

The year 1928 saw the last public duty performed by Sir William Boyd Dawkins, the opening in September of the new Buxton Public Library and Museum. Very aptly his opening address was upon cave exploration in Derbyshire, and the Museum appropriately devoted three of its six available rooms to displays of the important Peak District cave collections from Cresswell Crags, Longcliffe, Dove Holes, Deepdale, and elsewhere, arranged by Mr. G. H. Hill, the first Librarian and Curator in these new premises. Many benefactors to the new Museum attended the opening to hear Sir William, including W. H. Salt, F. A. Holmes, H. R. P. Lomas, and Alderman Dr. H. H. Bemrose who proposed a vote of thanks which was seconded by J. Wilfrid Jackson. Jackson's relationship with Buxton was very close from this time on, being elected an honorary member of the Buxton Archaeological and Natural History Society in 1928, and in the following year he was appointed an 'Honorary Consultant' to Buxton Museum.

Opening of the Boyd Dawkins Room, 30th October, 1929. Left to right: seated Sir Arthur Evans and Dr. Jackson, standing Mr. W. Salt, and Buxton Museum Curator, Mr. G. H. Hill. Photo: Buxton Museum.

Dawkins' encouraging words on opening Buxton Museum regarding its role and future bore fruits at an early stage, for upon his death in January 1929 Sir William bequeathed to Buxton Museum his library and scientific manuscripts. Lady Mary Boyd Dawkins discussed this bequest with Buxton's Deputy Mayor, Councillor J. J. E. Pugh, and the conclusion reached was that a special reference room be allocated for the collection, called the Boyd Dawkins Room. The original Boyd Dawkins Room was opened on 31st October 1929, by Sir Arthur Keith with support from Sir Arthur Evans, and Professor A. Sayce, and attracted considerable public attention with such distinguished names attached to the opening. Following the war, the contents of the original Boyd Dawkins room outgrew the available space and were moved to the first floor, and were later relegated to the storerooms. 1982 saw the restitution of the

Boyd Dawkins Room, which is also dedicated to Dr. Jackson, whose daughter in a similar manner presented his library and archives to the Museum.

To return to Jackson's inter-war activities, we enter, following the opening of Buxton Museum, his most active decade of work 1928-1938, which understandably was curtailed by the outbreak of the Second War. Without doubt his main activities during these years were excavating caves and open archaeological sites, and reporting on the bones and molluscs from these and other sites as his publications bear witness.

Jackson's most numerous field activities 1928-1930 were to the Settle caves which finally led to him giving the opening address to the new Settle Museum in 1931, and to the Prestatyn caves, which he excavated, and which like the Settle caves provided him with much material for lectures and talks. He also visited every year from 1928 to 1936 Northern Ireland during which time he was actively excavating the Ballintoy caves 1933-6, which yielded abundant and important evidence of human occupation. His excavations at Ballintoy were published in several numbers of the Irish Naturalist's Journal.

In between these activities Jackson undertook his most important field work abroad, for in 1931 he was invited by Dr. (later Sir) Robert Mond to assist in the Egypt Exploration Society excavations. Jackson was backed as a candidate to join the excavations by his close association with people like Sir Arthur Keith and Professor Fleure, and following his interview with Dr. Mond and O. H. Myers regarding his joining the excavations, the Manchester Museum granted in June 1931 his leave of absence. The summer of 1931 must have been spent in a wave of excited anticipation for Jackson, with frequent visits to and from Professor Fleure and Lady Boyd Dawkins regarding his Egyptian visit, and contact with many leading archaeologists and anthropologists including Sir Mortimer Wheeler, Sir A. S. Woodward, Dr. H. Wellcome and Lady Petrie, as a result of attending various functions prior to his leaving Britain.

Jackson sailed for Port Said on 21st November, and was to return on 22nd February the following year (1932). His job

Dr. Jackson in Egypt, 1931. From December 1931 to February 1932 he was engaged in excavating in the Armant and Tel el Amarna areas under the Egypt Exploration Society. Photo: Buxton Museum.

in Egypt was to work and report upon the animal remains, particularly sacred cattle, found in the burials near Armant, Upper Egypt, and to assist in the identification of human remains and other objects found in Predynastic graves. He was working in the field under Oliver Myers mainly in the Armant area and at the Bucheum in particular, and near the end of his stay at Tel el Amarna. His work during the excavations was wide ranging, for he not only dealt with animal remains and many human skulls, but was also busy working on flint artefacts and on repairing the antiquities recovered. Jackson naturally made the most of his time in Egypt by visiting all the classic sites at Gizah, Karnak, Luxor, Saqqara, etc., and of course the greatest discovery of the day in

Egypt, the tomb of Tutankhamen. During his visit Jackson actually met Howard Carter, who was rounding off his work in connection with the Tutankhamen discoveries, and Jackson witnessed the last crates leaving the tomb for the Cairo Museum.

The results of Jackson's work in Egypt appeared as specialist reports in Myers' monographs on Armant and the Bucheum, and as with all of his more important undertakings Jackson was to draw upon his experiences in Egypt in lectures and demonstrations for many years to come. For the short time that he was directly involved with Egyptian archaeology he came into direct contact with nearly all the leading figures in the subject from Howard Carter, Sir William and Lady Flinders Petrie, to Dr. Margaret Murray and Sir Robert Mond. Indeed, Jackson would have returned to the excavations of the Egypt Exploration Society, but for the critical illness suffered by his wife in the 1930's, and the deterioration in the health of his mother, who died in 1936 (the same year as Jackson's close friend, Robert Welch died).

Following his return from Egypt Jackson was busier than ever, attending conferences as the Museum's delegate (n.b. the B.A. at York 1932, the 1932 International Congress of Pre and Protohistory, the 1934 International Congress of Anthropology & Ethnological Sciences), lecturing (n.b. at the Manchester Egyptian & Oriental Society 1932, at the Royal Anthropological Institute 1933) and excavating (n.b. Ballintoy 1933-6). In all his activities he maintained his close contact with various provincial and national societies, and was elected in 1932 an Honorary Member of the Ancient Monuments Society (and a member of its executive council), in 1933 President of the North East Lancashire Naturalists

Excavations at Park Cave, Ballintoy, N. Ireland 14th April 1933. Dr. Jackson on the left led the excavations and J. K. Charlesworth joined the excavations (standing in cave at back). Photo: Buxton Museum.

Union and President of the Lancashire and Cheshire Antiquarian Society (in its 50th year), in 1934 an Honorary Member of the Belfast Naturalists Field Club and from 1934 onwards a permanent member of the General Committee of the British Association. He was further awarded in 1933 the Diploma of the Museums Association, and in 1934 received the Murchison Award of the Geological Society of London for his geological research of North Derbyshire and Dovedale.

As well as his reports on the Egyptian excavations, Jackson worked on a vast number of animal remains from a wide range of archaeological sites in Britain in the 1930's, many of which were published in monographs on the respective sites. Amongst this work were reports on the classic sites of Wilbury Camp, Grimes Graves, Old Sarum, Stonehenge, Avebury, Mildenhall, Bury Hill etc. Jackson's expertise in the identification of animal remains spread very widely in the 1930's, such that his services in this field were still being sought for major archaeological reports in the 1960's, and obviously as a result he came into contact with all the leading workers in archaeology in the 1930's, 40's and 50's, notably Wheeler, Woolley, the Hawkeses, Piggot, and Kendrick. A particularly strong link was established in the 1930's with Dr. Arthur Bulleid, with whom Jackson and Dawkins had previously been associated during the Glastonbury excavations. The centre of their interest in the 30's was the Burtle Beds of Somerset, which Bulleid had investigated at a number of sites. Jackson joined Bulleid in the study of these interesting deposits using his special knowledge of conchology and animal remains, and the results of their study appeared in the important joint papers in 1937 and 1941. Jackson visited

The first British Spelaeological Association Conference, Buxton, 27th July, 1936. Right to left: A. L. Armstrong, unknown, A. H. Ogilvie, Sir Arthur Keith, Dr. J. W. Jackson, E. Simpson, Miles Burkitt, J. W. Puttrell, Mr. Blackburn. Photo: Buxton Museum.

Bulleid many times in the 30's and struck a close friendship, and a substantial correspondence exists in Jackson's archive between them.

The 1930's were important in the caving world, for in 1935 the British Spelaeological Association was founded at Buxton, at which meeting Jackson was a founder member. In July 1936 the B.S.A. held its first conference, which was also in Buxton, and was attended by many important personalities such as Lady Boyd Dawkins, Sir Arthur Keith, Miles Burkitt and Dr. McCurdy, (see photograph). A special exhibition was opened by Lady Boyd Dawkins, and the delegates visited Pooles Cavern, Buxton and Cresswell Crags under Dr. Jackson's leadership. The B.S.A.'s first President was Sir Arthur Keith, while Jackson himself was to become its President in 1964, and played a very important role in furthering the Association. Upon the foundation of the B.S.A. Jackson was immediately involved in compiling a 'Schedule of Cave Finds' for the Association, a massive task involving contacting every establishment in the country with collections of cave material, which was partially published in *Caves and Caving*.

The war years once again brought with them fundamental changes. Jackson was appointed in August 1939 an Operations and Intelligence Officer based in Manchester, and his services in this capacity were especially sought during the Manchester air raids 1940-1942. When not on War Room duty Jackson was busily engaged at the Manchester Museum packing up type and other specimens for storage to avoid bomb damage. His fieldwork and travelling were naturally much restricted in the war years, and most travelling he did undertake was to areas local to Manchester, especially Buxton, where he made many visits to see F. A. Holmes with whom he had had close contact over Dovedale.

Jackson maintained through the war years a healthy correspondence with his colleagues in geology, archaeology and conchology, and maintained close contact with the many societies he was attached to. He was elected President of several societies in the war years, namely the Buxton Archaeological and Natural History Society in 1940, the Lancashire & Cheshire Fauna Committee, the N.W. Federation of Museums & Art Galleries, and the Yorkshire Naturalists Union in 1943, and the Liverpool Geological Society in 1945. Jackson was also elected a life Fellow of the Society of Antiquaries in 1939, and vice-president of the Youth Hostels Association in 1938, all of which demonstrate the wide appreciation of his work.

Jackson's research work during the war continued along established lines with a series of bone reports for various archaeological sites, amongst which the most important was Maiden Castle which had been excavated by Sir Mortimer Wheeler in the years before the war. Jackson also used some of the additional research time that was available to him, to undertake biographical studies into the work of two early naturalists, Captain Thomas Brown and Martin Lister, which were published in 1944 and 1945.

The end of the war marked the end of and the beginning of old and new chapters in Dr. Jackson's life. On V.E. Day, 8th May 1945 he was on a visit to Maiden Castle and Stonehenge, and by September of the same year Jackson had retired from Manchester Museum and was living in Buxton. His last curatorial job at Manchester was the sorting and removal from Macclesfield of the fossil collections of his and Sir William Boyd Dawkins' old friend Sir Arthur Smith Woodward who had died in 1944.

In moving to Buxton, Jackson was in the middle of an area that was close to his heart in its geological and archaeological interests, and yet within easy reach of his old base at Manchester. Retirement was hardly an appropriate term in describing Jackson's life after his career in Manchester, for he launched in 1946 into a hive of activity that lasted at least another thirty years!

Jackson's post war research continued with a steady stream of publications into the 1960's. He was called upon to report on many archaeological sites yielding animal remains, including the important sites of Little Woodbury, Colchester, St. Albans, and Bagendon, and he published some important papers on caves, including Sun Hole 1955, Victoria Caves 1964, and Cresswell Caves 1967. Jackson's most outstanding publications of these post war years are probably his catalogue of the type and figured specimens in the Geology Department of Manchester Museum (1952), and his chapter on Archaeology and Palaeontology in the book British Caving (1953 and 1962). His catalogue of type and figured specimens was the gathering together of years of research on the geological collections at Manchester during his term as curator there, and was and still is the most important publication relating to the Museum's geological collections. Jackson's contribution to British Caving was likewise a most significant piece of work which brought together for the first time since Dawkins' Cave Hunting all the historical background and knowledge to date relating to the archaeology and palaeontology of every bone-cave in Great Britain. As others have remarked, in the book's successor 'The Science of Speleology' published in 1976 it took four authors to tackle the same subject matter as Jackson, producing only half as much text!

Towards the end of the war Jackson began to take a series of W.E.A. classes in geology, and he continued teaching W.E.A. classes until 1971. In the late 1940's he was taking classes in Manchester, Stockport, Buxton and Chapel, and by the late 1950's was taking classes in Manchester and Buxton. In the 1960's when he was in his eighties he was still running his Buxton W.E.A. classes, and in 1966 was elected the first President of the Buxton Branch of the W.E.A. which had become a nationally organised body.

Jackson occupied the post war years into the 1960's with a wealth of lectures and field excursions, mostly attached to various societies of which he was or had been a leading officer, notably the Manchester Geologists' Association, the Liverpool Geological Society, the Lancashire and Cheshire Antiquarian Society, the Buxton Archaeological and Natural History Society, and the Buxton Field Club. As well as being prominent in these societies he was very active in the post war years on the councils of bodies such as the National Trust Dovedale Local Committee (honorary Secretary (1945-1958), the Buxton Library and Museum Committee (1947-1952), the Council for the Protection of Rural England (elected local President

Manchester Geologists' Association and Buxton Field Club excursion to Stoney Middleton Dale, 17th August, 1958. Dr. Jackson, centre right, leader. Photo: L. Williamson.

1953), the Council for British Archaeology, and the Peak Park Planning Board (1956-1961).

Further honours were made to him in the post war years by societies, notably in 1948 with the presentation of the Liverpool Geological Society's Medal, Honorary memberships to the N.W. Federation of Museums & Art Galleries (1946), the Altrincham & District Natural History & Literary Society (1946), the Lancashire and Cheshire Fauna Committee (1948), the Manchester Literary & Philosophical Society (1954), the Conchological Society (1955), and the Vice Presidency to the Prehistoric Society (1946). Over and above these societies, he even made new contacts such as with the Derbyshire Archaeological Society, and the Peakland Archaeological Society, and from 1956 to 1962 ran the Bangor Summer School in geology.

Sadly for Jackson, he saw many colleagues of long standing from the early days pass away, men such as Welch, Bulleid, Balch, Kennard and Keith, all of whom he outlived for many years. He also suffered two most painful personal blows, first the death in 1952 of his wife Alicia and in 1977 the death of his son Robert which worsened his own health until he died on 16th November 1978 and was buried next to his wife in St. Peter's Churchyard, Fairfield, Buxton.

Dr. Jackson can be much admired for his great strength of mind and body when one considers how mentally as well as physically active he was in his 90's. In 1976 at the age of 96 he for instance conducted a Buxton Archaeological Society Presidential tour to the Wildboarclough area of the Peak District, and in the same year layed the foundation stone for the new Poole's Cavern Interpretation Centre in Buxton. Such undertakings in his advanced years were highly regarded by the local societies he was attached to, and for them Dr. Jackson was a living link with a whole generation of early archaeologists who had become historical figures to the younger generation.

Dr. Jackson, living the long and active life he did, was indeed one of our few remaining contemporary naturalists who had had firm links with the last of the classical Victorian naturalists. His close association with Sir William Boyd Dawkins for instance was also a secondary link with such men as Sir Charles Lyell, Thomas Huxley, John Phillips and Charles Darwin, with whom Dawkins was acquainted. Jackson himself had a great sense of history, and his association with many other naturalists particularly in the field of conchology, often led him to write their obituary notices and historical papers which have become valuable biographical references. In his own studies Dr. Jackson was 'a systematics man', providing as he did identifications of a wide range of animals especially mammals, molluscs and brachiopods, often for the use of others. Dr. Jackson had less flare for theory then Dawkins, and certainly did not chase the limelight of arcaheological discovery and debate that Dawkins had a weakness for. We must I believe place Dr. Jackson above Sir William Boyd Dawkins as a palaeontologist when one looks at the very exact and systematic way that Jackson treats his subject matter, even allowing for the pioneering days that Dawkins was working in. At the end of the day a scientist's worth lies in his powers of recording data correctly, and a critical look at Dawkins' work often uncovers inexactness and mistakes which Jackson can be rarely accused of. We have in Jackson one of those very keen men who delighted in the pursuit of natural science as a hobby, and with hardly any formal training, had the motivation to turn their hobby into a lifelong career without seeking any self-advancement in their position, career-wise or socially.

BIBLIOGRAPHY

The following contains all of Dr. Jackson's contributions to scientific journals, except in some cases, a few bone reports which were submitted to other authors and their publication has not been traced. Also omitted are Dr. Jackson's many contributions to newspapers, magazines and society newsletters, and some periodicals of small provincial societies.

CONCHOLOGY (incl. RECENT BRACHIOPODA)

1902 Report on the Hope and Castleton Ramble. *J. Conchology,* X, p.141, 216

1903 Notes on the Miller's Dale Ramble. August 9th 1902, *Ibid.,* p.303

1903 *Helix rotundata* Müll. m. *sinistrosum* at Castleton, Derbyshire. *Ibid.,* p.284

1904 Report on the Miller's Dale Ramble. *Ibid.,* 11, p.105

1904 Report on the Fleetwood Ramble. *Ibid.,* p.115

1904 Report on the Miller's Dale Ramble. *Ibid.,* p.13

1904 with TAYLOR, F. Observations on the habits and reproduction of *Paludestrina taylori. Ibid.,* p.9-11

1904 and MOORE, C. H. Further Observations on the Molluscan Fauna of Grange-over-Sands, Lancs., and District. *Ibid.,* p.45-47

1905 *Pisidum nitidum* var. *splendens* in West Lancashire. *Ibid.,* p.170

1906 *Vertigo alpestrias* in Westmorland. *Ibid.,* p.359

1906 Further notes on French Shell Names. *Ibid.,* p.359

1906 *Bulimus fasciatus* Turton [= *Helicella barbara* (L)] in Lancashire. *Ibid.,* p.367

1906 The Occurrence of the white form of *Helicigona lapicida* (L). *Ibid.,* p.345

1906 An Attempt to breed from a sinistral *Helix pomatia,* with notes on the reproduction of the Dart. *Ibid.,* p.341-345

1906 *Acanthinula lamellata* (Jeff) at Grange-over-Sands, Lancs., and Notes on various other species. *Ibid.,* p.361

1907 Notes on *Succinea oblonga* Drap., and other species at Grange-over-Sands, Lancs. *The Naturalist,* May, p.173-174

1907 *Vitrea cellaria* in Shell-Marl, near Hale, Westmorland. *ibid.,* August, p.280

1907 with KENNARD, A. S. On the Discovery of *Vitrea rogersi* in England. *J. Conchology,* 12, p.63

1907-8 Bibliography of the Non-Marine Mollusca of Lancashire. *Ibid.,* p.49-54, 69-79, 124-128, 147-156, 218-219

1908 Notes on Cheshire Land and Freshwater Mollusca. *The Naturalist,* Dec., p.436

1908 *Helicella barbara* (L) in Lancashire. *J. Conchology,* 12, p.106

1908 Report of the Grange Ramble, June 10th, 1908. *Ibid.,* p.221-222

1909 On the Mollusca from the 'Cave-earth'', Dog Holes, Warton Crag. *Lancs. Naturalist,* Dec., p.217-22, 233-238, 261-265

1909 Holocene Mollusca near Great Mitton, West Yorkshire. *J. Conchology,* 12, p.263-265

1909 Mollusca of Kendal, Westmorland. *Ibid.,* p.310-315

1909 On a Fossil Dart and Epiphragm of *Helix pomatia* found in the Loess deposit of the Rhine Valley. *Ibid.,* 12, p.265

1909 with KENNARD, A. S. On the former occurrence of *Unio (Margaritana) margaritifer* Linné in the River Thames. *Ibid.,* p.321-322

1910 A double-mouthed *Clausilia bidentata* at Yealand Conyers, near Carnforth, Lancs. *Lancs. Naturalist,* Nov., p.275-276

1910 Further notes on Double-mouthed species of *Clausiliae. Lancs. Naturalist,* Dec. p.307

1910 Notes on Shropshire Mollusca. *Ibid.,* 13, p.46-47

1910 On the habitat of *Vitrea lucida* (Drap.) at Grange-over-Sands. *Ibid.,* p.65-68

1910 *Pyramidula rotundata* var. *alba* at Meathop Fell, Westmorland. *Ibid.,* p.124

1911 On the occurrence of *Unio sinuatus* Lam. in the British Isles. *Ibid.,* p.142-143

1911 A double-mouthed *Clausilia bidentata* near Warton, West Lancashire. *Ibid.*, p.161

1912 On the Former Range of *Pomatias elegans* in the Warton District, *Lancs. Naturalist,* Aug., p.170-171

1912 The Brachiopoda of the Scottish National Antarctic Expedition. *Trans. R. Soc. Edinburgh,* XLVIII, p.367-390, plates I, II

1912 *Cypraea pantherina* (Solander M S), Dillwyn, in Saxon Graves. *J. Conchology,* 13, p.307-308

1912 *Pisidium amnicum* (Müll) near Hale, Westmorland. *Ibid.*, p.311

1912 *Jaminia secale* (Drap.) near Penrith, Cumberland. *Ibid.*, p.313

1913 *Helix nemoralism* sinistrosum in West Kent. *Ibid.*, 14, p.41

1913 Conchologists at Castleton, *Lancs. Naturalist,* Oct., p.245-247

1913 On the presence of Shell-fragments in Prehistoric Pottery. *Ibid.*, Dec., p.321-322

1913 with STANDEN, R. Observations on the non-marine mollusca of Prestatyn, North Wales, *Ibid.*, p.346-357

1914 On *Helicella crayfordensis. Proc. Malac. Soc.*, XI, p.270 (not seen)

1914 Notes on the candidula section of *Helicella. J. Conchology,* 14, p.193-199

1914 *Caecilioides acicula, Vallonia excentrica,* etc., in Denbighshire. *Ibid.*, p.231

1914 Holocene Mollusca from Clapham, Yorkshire. *The Naturalist,* Apr. p.121-2

1914 with BOYCOTT, A. E. A Note on the Apparent Absence of Sexual Characters in the Shell of *Neritina fluviatalis. Annals Mag. Nat. Hist.*, XIV, p.369-375

1914 with BOYCOTT, A. E. Observations on the anatomy of *Helicella 'heripensis* Mabille'. *J. Conchology,* 14, p.164-168

1915 Notes on the collection and preservation of the Non-marine Mollusca of Lancashire and Cheshire. *Lancs. & Cheshire Naturalist,* May p.1-3

1915 Report on the Mollusca. *Ibid.*, p.40-43

1915 *Pisidium supinum.* A Schdmidt in South Lancashire. *Ibid.*, p.67

1915 with BOYCOTT, A. E. A further note on pigmentation in *Helicella gigaxii. J. Conchology,* 14, p.304-305

1916 The Geographical Distribution of the use of Pearls and Pearl-shell. *Mem. & Proc. Manch. Lit. & Phil. Soc.*, 60, No. 12, p.1-53

1916 The Use of Cowry-shells for the Purposes of Currency, Amulets, and Charms. *Ibid.*, No. 13, p.1-72

1916 The Money Cowry *(Cypraea moneta* L.*)* as a Sacred Object among North American Indians. *Ibid.*, No. 41, p.1-10

1916 The Aźtec Moon Cult and its relation to the Chank-cult of India. *Ibid.*, No. 5, p.1-5

1916 The Geographical Distribution of the Shell-Purple Industry. *Ibid.*, No. 7, p.1-29

1916 Shell Trumpets and their Distribution in the Old and New World. *Ibid.*, No. 8, p.1-22

1916 Report on the Mollusca. *Lancs. & Cheshire Naturalists,* June, p.74-76

1916 Pre-Columbian Use of the Money Cowrie in America. *Nature,* Sept. 21

1917 Shells as Evidence of the Migrations of Early Culture. Manchester University Press

1917 Report on the Mollusca. *Lancs. & Cheshire Naturalist,* June, p.80

1917 *Helicella virgata* (Da Costa) in Wirral, Cheshire. *J. Conchology,* 15, p.203

1918 *Limnaea glabra* var. *albida* nov. and *Planorbis vortex* var. *albida* nov. *Ibid.*, p.288

1918 Thread-spinning in *Physa heterostropha. Ibid.*, p.288

1918 *Limnaea glabra* in Ireland? *Irish Naturalist,* XXVII, p.77

1918 Report on the Mollusca. *Lancs. & Cheshire Naturalist,* June, p.69-72

1918 British Antarctic (Terra Nova) Expedition 1910. Brachiopoda. *British Museum (Natural History) Zoology,* II, p.177-202

1919 Rare shells in shell-pockets on the Wirral Sand-Dunes. *J. Conchology,* 16, p.68, plate 1

1919 'Shell-Pockets' on Sand-Dunes on the Wirral Coast, Cheshire; and Notes on Ancient Land Surfaces. *Lancs. & Cheshire Naturalist,* Jul.-Aug., p.9-14, 39-44

1919 with J. G. KITCHIN *Planorbis dilatatus* and *Physa heterostropha* in the River Tame, at Dukinfield, Cheshire. *Ibid.*, Nov. p.131-2

1920 Anodons in Whitworth Park Lake, Manchester. *Ibid.*, XIII, p.94

1920 The Association of Freshwater Mollusca and Crustacea. *Ibid.,* p.91-94

1920 Mollusca. Report for 1919. *Ibid.,* p.305-7

1921 Report on the Non-Marine Mollusca for 1920. *Ibid.,* p.213-4

1921 On the Occurrence of Lisitanian Brachiopods in the Persian Gulf. *Anns. Mag. Nat. Hist.,* VII, p.40-49

1922 On the Tufaceious Depositis of Caerwys, Flintshire and the Mollusca contained therein. *Lancs. & Cheshire Naturalist,* Feb., p.147-158

1925 The distribution of *Margaritana margarifera* in the British Isles. *J. Conchology,* 17, p.195-211, 270-278, plate 2

1926 Mollusca from Ancient Egyptian tombs. *The Naturalist,* Nov., p.338-340

1927 *Tonna (=Dolium) fasciata* (Brug.), with two pre-apertural varices; and notes on other forms. *J. Conchology,* 18, p.75-78

1928 Shells in Ancient Egyptian tombs. *The Naturalist,* June, p.175-6

1934 *Cypraea vinosa* Gmelin in a Saxon Woman's Grave in Somerset. *J. Conchology,* 20, p.46-47

1936 Mollusca. *Year Book N.W. Nats. Union,* p.25-32

1936 with N. FISHER. Early Records of Lancashire non-marine Mollusca by James Wright Whitehead. *J. Conchology,* 20, p.275-281

1937 with G. STIASNY. The Brachiopoda of the Siboga Expedition. Results of the Siboga Expedition, Monograph XXVII, Leiden 1937, p.1-20, 2 plates

1941 *Pisidia* of Lancashire and Cheshire. *J. Conchology,* 21, p.304-318

1944 Report on the Non-Marine Mollusca for 1937-42. *Lancs. & Cheshire Fauna Committee,* 26th Report, p.7-10

1944 Report on Marine Shells. In G. C. THOMSON The Tombs and Moon Temple of Hureidha. *Rep. Res. Comm. Soc. Antiq., No. XIII, p.104-105*

1952 A revision of Some South African Brachipoda, with Descriptions of new species. *Anns. S. African Museum,* XLI, p.1-40, plates I-III

1962 Land and Freshwater Mollusca. In D. E. OWEN et al. Fauna of the Manchester Area. *British Association,* 6, p.106-7

GEOLOGY

1905 with DEAN, J. D. Notes on a Chara and Shell-Marl Deposit at Hawes Water, Silverdale, Lancashire. *J. Conchology,* 11, p.147-151

1908 Mottled Foraminiferous Limestone in West and North Lancashire. *Geol. Mag.,* V, p.266-8

1908 Carboniferous fish-remains in North Derbyshire. *Ibid.,* V, p.309-310

1909 On the Type-specimen of *Pseudomelania vittata* (Phillips). *Ibid.,* VI, p.542-3

1909 Some fossil Pearl-growths. *Proc. Malacological Soc.,* VIII, 318-320, plate XIV

1910 On the Discovery of *Archaeosigillaria vanuxemi* (Göppert) at Meathop Fell, Westmorland, with a description of the locality. *Geol. Mag.,* VII, p.78-81

1910 Note on the discovery of a fish-spine in the Carboniferous Limestone at Clitheroe. *Lancs. Naturalist,* Sept. p.213, plate VI

1911 Remarks on some *Palaeoxyris* from the Middle Coal Measures of Lancashire. *Ibid.,* Jan., p.325-332, plates X, XI

1911 *Strophodus* teeth in the Corallian Beds of Malton. *Ibid.,* Apr., p.151

1911 A new species of *Unio* from the Yorkshire Estuarine Series with notes on other forms. *The Naturalist,* June, p.211-214, plate XIV

1911 On *Unio distortus* Bean, and *Alasmodom vetustus* Brown, from the Upper Estuarine Beds of Gristhorpe, Yorks. *Ibid.,* Feb.-Mar. p.104-107, 119-122, plates IX, X

1911 Palaeontological Notes from the Manchester Museum. *Archaeocidaris* in the Middle Coal Measures of Lancashire; with notes on other species. *Geol. Mag.,* VIII, p.403-406

1912 Palaeontological Notes from the Manchester Museum: or Mollusca from the Lancashire Coal Measures. *Ibid.,* IX, p.449-453

1912 Cambrian Fossils. *Lancs. Naturalist,* Oct., p.247

1914 Notes on Shell-Marl deposits in N. Lancashire and Westmorland. *Lancs. & Cheshire Naturalist,* July-August, p.135-140, 197-201

1916 Brachipod Morphology: Notes and Comments on Dr. J. Allan Thomson's Papers. *Geol. Mag.*, III, p.21-6

1918 On the new Brachiopod Genus, *Liothyrella,* of Thomson. *Ibid.*, V, p.73-9

1918 The Association of faceted pebbles with glacial deposits. *Mem. & Proc. Manch. Lit. & Phil. Soc.*, 62, p.1-13, plates I, II

1918 On a New Carboniferous Nautiloid *(Coelonautilus trapezoidalis). Mem. & Proc. Manch. Lit. & Phil. Soc.*, 63, p.1-4

1919 On the occurence of *Productus humerosus (=sublaevus)* in Dove Dale; and its value as a Zone-fossil. *Geol. Mag.*, VI, p.507-9

1919 and H. K. and S. G. BRADE-BIRKS. Notes on Myriopoda. A revision of some fossil material from Spath Bottoms, Lancs. *Ibid.*, p.406-11, plate IX

1920 The Quartzose Conglomerate at Caldon Law, Staffordshire. *Ibid.*, LVII, p.487-492

1922 On the occurrence of *Daviesiella llangollensis* (Dav.) in Derbyshire. *Ibid.*, LIX, p.461-8

1923 *Calamites (Calamitina) göpperti* Ett. at Hebden Bridge Yorks. *The Naturalist,* July, p.233-5

1923 On the correlation of Yoredales and Pendlesides. *Ibid.*, Oct. p.337-8

1924 Notes on some 'Pendleside' fossils. *Ibid.*, p.307-8

1925 On the occurrence of *Conularia* in the Carboniferous Limestone of North Wales. Mem. & Proc. Manch. Lit. & Phil. Soc., LXIX, p.1-4

1925 The Relation of the Edale Shales to the Carboniferous Limestone in North Derbyshire. *Geol. Mag.*, LXII, p.267-274

1925 Sabden Shale Fossils near Holywell, Flintshire. *The Naturalist,* June, p.183-4

1926 The Goniatite zones below the Kinder Scout Grit in North Derbyshire. *Ibid.*, July, p.205-207

1926 The Geological Collection in Manchester Museum. *The Old Owensian Journal,* IV, p.25-30

1926 with O. T. JONES. Facetted Pebbles in the South Manchester District. *Mem. & Proc. Manch. Lit. & Phil. Soc.*, 70, p.125-132

1927 The succession below the Kinder Scout Grit in North Derbyshire. *J. Manch. Geol. Assn.*, 1, p.15-32

1927 New Carboniferous Lamellibranchs and Notes on other forms. *Mem. & Proc. Manch. Lit. & Phil. Soc.*, 71, p.93-122

1927 Geology of the Peak District. Ramblers Federation Handbook

1928 with J. PRINGLE. *Tylonautilus nodiferus* gen. nov. = *Nautilus (Discites) nodiferus* Armstrong. *The Naturalist,* Dec., p.373-378, plate XI

1929 *Goniatites spiralis* in a section near the North Craven fault, Settle district. *The Naturalist,* Jan., p.57-8

1930 Problems in the Classification of the Carboniferous Rocks. *J. Manch. Geol. Assn.*, 1, p.63-78

1934 The Geology and Geography of the Peak District. Handbook Nat. Assn. Head Teachers, p.48-56

1934 with A. E. TRUEMAN. Notes on the Lower Coal Measure Fossils from Messrs. Jarmain's boring, Kirkheaton near Huddersfield. *Summ. Prog. Geol. Surv. G.B.*, Part II, p.45-49

1934 Marine Fossils from the Lower Coal Measures near Huddersfield. *Ibid.*

1938 with A. BULLEID. The Burtle Sand Beds of Somerset. *Proc. Som. Arch. & Nat. Hist. Soc.*, LXXXIII, p.171-195, plates XXVII-XXXIII

1941 Description of a Carboniferous Limestone Section with *Girvanella* in North Derbyshire. *J. Manch. Geol. Assn.*, I, p.239-246

1941 *Spirifer bollandensis* Muir-Wood at Thorpe Cloud, with notes on the sequence in Dove Dale, Derbyshire. *Ibid.*, p.233-237

1942 with A. BULLEID. Further notes on the Burtle Beds of Somerset. *Proc. Som. Arch. & Nat. Hist. Soc.*, LXXXVII, p.111-116

1946 *Tylonautilus nodiferus* (Armstrong) from the Cefn & Fedw Series at Nant-Y-Ffrith (New to North Wales). *Proc. Liv. Geol. Soc.*, XIX, p.161-4

1947 The Upper Pleistocene fauna and its relation to the Ice Age. *Ibid.*, p.165-183

1948 Progress in Carboniferous Geology: The Millstone Grit Series. *Ibid.*, XX, p.1-22

1952 Catalogue of Types and Figures Specimens in the Geological Department of the Manchester Museum. *Manch. Mus. Pub.* No. 6, pp.i-vii, 1-170

1953 *Reticuloceras reticulatum* mut. *superbilingue* Bisat at Combs, near Chapel-en-le-Frith, Derbyshire. *Liverpool & Manch. Geol. Journ.*, 1, p.191-3

1958 *Lonsdaleia* in the Eyam Limestone at Mill Lane, Eyam, Derbyshire. *Ibid.*, 2, p.81

1958 Further records of *Reticuloceras reticulatum* mut. *superbilingue* in the Combs Valley, near Chapel-en-le-Frith, Derbyshire. *Ibid.*, p.80

1958 *Daviesiella llangollensis* (Davidson) at Lean Low, Near Parsley Hay, Derbyshire. *Ibid.*, p.70

1959 with R. M. C. EAGAR and F. M. BROADHURST. The Area around Manchester. Geologists' Assn. Guide No. 7, p.28-32

1960 The Geology and Scenery of the Peak District and Adjacent Areas. Handbook Nat. Assn. Head Teachers, p.23-29

1970 with F. M. BROADHURST et al. Geologists' Association Guide No. 7, Revised Edition, p.8-13

1971 Geological Structure and Scenery. Peak District National Park Guide, No. 3

1972 Edale. In F. W. COPE. The Peak District. Geologists' Association Guide, No. 26, 2nd Edn., p.31-35

CAVES

1909 Notes on the Bone-Caves of Grange and District. *Lancs. Naturalist,* June, p.86-93

1909 On the Discovery of the Remains of Lemmings in Dog Holes, Warton Crag. *Ibid.,* Dec., p.227-9

1910 Preliminary Report on the Exploration of 'Dog Holes' Cave, Warton Crag, near Carnforth, Lancashire. *Trans. Lancs. & Cheshire Antiq. Soc.,* XXVII, p.1-32, plate I & II

1910 On the Vertebrate fauna found in the Cave-earth at Dog Holes, Warton Crag. *Lancs. Naturalist,* Feb., p.322-332

1910 The vertebrate fauna found in the Cave-earth at Dog Holes, Warton Crag (Lancashire). *Proc. Geol. Soc. Lond.* (Abstracts), No. 887, p.49-50

1911 Further Report on the Explorations at Dog Holes, Warton Crag, Lancs., with remarks on the contents of two adjacent caves. *Trans. Lancs. & Cheshire Antiq. Soc.,* XXVIII, p.59-81, plates I & II

1912 Additional notes on the Pleistocene Fauna of Dog Holes, Warton Crag. *Lancs. Naturalist,* March, p.420-422

1913 Report on the recent explorations at Dog Holes, Warton Crag. *Trans. Cumb. & West. Arch. Soc.,* XIII, p.55-58

1913 Third Report on the Explorations at Dog Holes, Warton Crag, Lancs. *Trans. Lancs. & Cheshire Antiq. Soc.,* XXX, p.99-130, 1 plate

1913 On the occurrence of the Lynx in North Wales and Derbyshire. *Geol. Mag.,* X, p.259-262

1913 Some Cave Notes. *Lancs. Naturalist,* April, p.39-40

1914 Report on the Exploration of a Cave at Haverbrack, Westmorland. *Trans. Cumb. & West. Antiq. & Archaeol. Soc.,* XIV, p.262-271

1924 Report on the Animal Remains found in Read's Cavern, near Burrington Combe, Somerset. *Proc. Univ. Bristol, Spelaeol. Soc.,* 2, p.55-58

1925 Report on the Animal Remains found at the cave known as Mother Grundy's Parlour, Cresswell. *J.R. Anthrop. Inst.,* LV, p.176-8

1926 Recent Cave Exploration in Derbyshire. *North West Naturalist,* Sept., p.129-196

1927 Chelm's Combe Shelter. The Vertebrate and Molluscan Fauna. *Proc. Somerset. Arch. Soc.,* 72, p.115-23

1928 Report on the Vertebrate Fauna from Bridged Pot Shelter, Ebbor, Somerset. *Rep. Wells Nat. Hist. & Archaeol. Soc.,* 1928, p.27-31

1929 Cresswell Caves. *Trans. Lancs. & Cheshire Antiq. Soc.,* XLIV, 7pp

1929 Remains of Lemmings in Derbyshire Caves. *The Naturalist,* March, p.105-107

1931 The Vertebrate and Molluscan Fauna of Soldier's Hole, Cheddar. *Proc. Som. Arch. & Nat. Hist. Soc.,* LXXVI, p.58-62

1931 Lynx Remains from Yorkshire Caves. *The Naturalist,*April

1932 with W. K. MATTINSON. A Cave on Giggleswick Scars, near Settle, Yorkshire. *Ibid.,* Jan., p.5-9

1932 The Vertebrate Fauna of Bridged Pot Cave, Ebbor Gorge, Somerset. *Rep. Wells Nat. Hist. & Archaeol. Soc.,* 1932, p.47-51

1933 Settle excavations: in M. KITSON CLARK, Roman Yorkshire, 1933, *J. Yorks Archaeol. Soc.,* XXXI, p.331

1933 Preliminary Report on Excavations at the Caves of Ballintoy, Co. Antrim. *Irish Nat. Journ.,* IV, 6pp

1934 Further Excavations at Ballintoy Caves, Co. Antrim. *Ibid.,* V, p.104-109, plate 6

1936 Excavations at Ballintoy Caves, Co. Antrim. Third Report, *Ibid.,* VI, p.31-42

1937 Cave-Hunting. *Trans Rochdale Lit. & Sci. Soc.,* XIX, p.72-81

1937-8 Schedule of Cave Finds. *Caves and Caving,* I, p.18-21, 48-51, 89-92, 127-130, 160

1938 Excavations at Ballintoy Caves, Co. Antrim. Fourth Report. *Irish Nat. Journ.* VII, p.107-112

1953 Archaeology and Palaeontology. Chapter VIII in C.H.D. CULLINGFORD (Ed.) British Caving, p.170-246

1955 The Pleistocene Vertebrate Fauna of Sun Hole, Cheddar. *Proc. Univ. Bristol. Spelaeol. Soc.,* 7, p.73-75

1962 Archaeology and Palaeontology. Chapter VII in C.H.D. CULLINGFORD (Ed.) British Caving, 2nd Edn., p.252-346

1964 Victoria and other local caves: a Biological and Archaeological Summary. *Proc. Brit. Speleol. Assn.* II, 5pp

1967 The Cresswell Caves. *Journn. Brit. Spelaeol. Assn.,* VI, p.8-23, 2 plates

BONE REPORTS

1913 Report on the Animal Remains found at the Roman Fort at Manchester. *Trans. Lancs. & Cheshire Antiq. Soc.,* XXXI, p.113-118

1915 Notes on the Vertebrate and Molluscan remains from Dyserth Castle. *Archaeologia Cambrensis,* Jan., p.77-82

1917 with W. B. DAWKINS. The Remains of the Mammalia found in the Lake Village of Glastonbury. Chapters XXV and XXVI & Appendix, in A. BULLEID & H.St. G. GRAY. The Glastonbury Lake Village, II, p.641-672, plate XCVII

1922 Report on Animal Remains from Thatcham, nr. Newbury. *Proc. Prehist. Soc.,* III, p.499

1923 Report on the Animal Remains found at Harborough Cave, Derbyshire. *Journ. R. Anthrop. Inst.,* LIII

1924 Report on the Animal Remains found at the Village Site at Fifield, Bavant Down. *Wilts. Archaeol. & Nat. Hist. Mag.,* XLII, p.492-3

1924 Note on the Animal Remains. In M. E. CUNNINGTON The Early Iron Age Inhabited Site at All Cánning Cross Farm, Wiltshire, p.43-50, plate 52

1925 Report on the Animal Remains from the Ancient Village Site of Swallocliffe Down, Wilts. *Wilts. Archaeol. & Nat. Hist. Mag.,* XLIII, p.90-93

1928 Bone report in: MARQUESS OF LANSDOWNE, A Roman Village at Nuthills, near Bowood. *Ibid.,* XLIV, p.6-7

1928 Report on the Animal Remains found in the Kilgreany Cave Co. Waterford. *Proc. Univ. Bristol Spelaeol. Soc.,* 3, p.137-153

1929 Report on the Animal Remains found at Woodhenge, Durrington, Wiltshire. In M. E. CUNNINGTON Woodhenge, p.61-69, plate 1

1930 Notes on Animal Remains found at the Chambered Cairn of Bryn Celli Ddu, Anglesey. *Archaeologia,* LXXX, p.195 and 213

1930 The Animal Remains found at Kingsdown Camp, Somerset. *Ibid.,* p.95-97

1931 Report on the Animal Remains from the 'Sanctuary', Overton Hill, near Avebury, *Wilts. Arch. & Nat. Hist. Mag.,* XIV, p.330-2

1932 Report on Animal Bones from the excavations of Merlin's Cave, Symond's Yat. *Proc. Univ. Bristol Spelaeol. Soc.,* 4, p.15-16

1932 Report on Animal Remains from Pare Dinmoor, Pennon, Anglesey. *Arch. Camb.,* Dec., p.252

1932 Report on Animal Remains from the Flint Mine Excavations 1930, Easton Down, Winterslow, S. Wilts. *Wilts. Arch. & Nat. Hist. Mag.,* XLV, p.362-3, 368-9

1932 The Vertebrate Fauna of Bridged Pot Shelter, Ebbor, Somerset. *Mendip Nature Res. Comm.*, Report 25, p.47-51

1932 Note on a few Animal Remains from Saxon Interments on Roche Court Down, Winterslow. *Wilts. Arch. & Nat. Hist. Mag.*, XIV, p.570

1933 Report on Animal Remains from the Flint Mine, Easton Down, Winterslow. *Ibid.*, XLVI, p.235

1933 Report on Animal Remains from an Early Bronze Age Site in the Fens near Cambridge. *Antiq. Journal,* XIII, p.278

1933 Report on the Animal Remains from the Roman Villa at Hucclecote, Gloucestershire. *Trans. Bristol & Glouc. Arch. Soc.*, 55, p.370-3

1933 Note on the Animal Remains from Almondsbury. *Proc. Univ. Bristol. Spelaeol. Soc.*, 4, p.138

1933 Report on the Animal Remains found at Meon Hill, near Stockbridge, Hampshire. *Proc. Hamps. F.C. & Arch. Soc.*, XIII, p.156-7

1934 Report on Animal Remains from a Pagan Saxon Settlement at Medmerry, Selsey. *Antiq. Journal,* XIV, p.394

1934 Notes on Animal Remains from the Neolithic Dwelling Pits at Winterbourne Dauntaey. *Wilts. Arch. & Nat. Hist. Mag.*, XLVI, p.446

1934 Report on the Remains of Sacred Cattle from the Baquria and Bucheum, Armant, Upper Egypt. Chapter XVII in Sir R. MOND & O. H. MYERS The Bucheum, I, Eygpt Exploration Society, p.137-142, plate XCVII (III)

1934 Report on Animal Remains from the Highfield Dwellings, Fisherton, Salisbury — *Wilts. Archaeol. & Nat. Hist. Mag.*, XLVI, p.619-624, 590 & 594

1934 Report on the Animal Remains from Whitehawk Camp, Brighton. *Antiq. Journal,* XIV, p.127-9

1935 Report on the Animal Remains from Pit 12 Grimes' Graves, Norfolk. *Proc. Prehist. Soc.*, VII, p.393-4

1935 Report on Animal Remains from the Neolithic Refuse Pit at Ratfyn, Amesbury, Wilts. *Wilts. Arch. & Nat. Hist. Mag.*, XLVII, p.61, 66-7

1935 Report on an Associated Skeleton of a Dog found with Beaker Pottery at Easton Down, Winterslow. *Wilts. Arch. & Nat. Hist. Mag.*, XLVII, p.76-8, plate 8

1935 Report on a collection of bones from a Tumulus on Warborough Hill, Stiffkey, Norfolk. *Norfolk & Norwich Arch. Soc.*, XXV, p.423

1935 Notes on Animal Remains from Hayes Wood Enclosure, Freshford, Somerset. *Proc. Som. Arch. & Nat. Hist. Soc.*, LXXXI, p.146

1935 Report on Animal Remains from the Chambered Cairn of Clettravel, N. Uist. *Proc. Soc. Antiq. Scot.;* LXIX, p.499

1935 Report on the Animal Remains found at Avebury Circle. *Archaeologia,* 84, p.157-9

1935 Report on Animal Remains found at Meon Hill, near Stockbridge, Hampshire. *Proc. Hamps. F.C. & Arch. Soc.*, XIII, p.39-42

1935 Report on the Animal Remains from the 11th century cesspit at Old Sarum. *Antiq. Journal,* XV, p.191-2

1935 Animal Remains from Recent Excavations at Peacock's Farm, Shippea Hill, Cambs. *Antiq. Journal,* XV, p.306

1935 The Animal Remains from the Stonehenge excavations of 1920-6. *Ibid.*, p.434-440

1936 Report on Animal Remains from a Late Bronze Age Site at Mildenhall, Cambridge. *Ibid.*, XVI, p.33-4

1936 Report on the Animal Remains from Whitehawk Camp, Brighton. *Sussex Archaeol. Col.*, LXXVII, p.88-90

1936 Report on the Animal Remains from Giant's Hill Long Barrow, Skendleby, Lincs. *Archaeolgia,* LXXXV, p.95-98

1936 Report on Animal Remains from Torrs Cave, Kirkcudbright. *Proc. Antiq. Soc. Scot.*, LXXI, p.415-30

1937 Animal Remains from an Enclosure on Boscombe Down of Late Bronze Age. *Wilts. Archaeol. & Nat. Hist. Mag.*, XLVII, p.484-6

1937 Animal Remains from a late Bronze Age Habitation Site on Thorny Down, Winterbourne Gunner, S. Wilts. *Ibid.*, p.659

1937 Report on Animal Remains from the Iron Age Site at Camerton. *Proc. Som. Arch. & Nat. Hist. Soc.*, LXXXIII, p.163-5

1937 Report on the Animal Remains from the Excavations at Julliberrie's Grave, Chilham, Kent. *Antiq. Journal,* XVII, p.133-5

1937 Report on the Human Remains, & Report on the Animal Remains, Chapters IX & XV in Sir R. MOND & O. H. MYERS Cemetaries of Armant I, Egypt Exploration Society, p.144-157, 254-258

1938 with E. K. TRATMAN. The Excavations of Backwell Cave, Somerset. *Proc. Univ. Bristol Spelaeol. Soc.,* 5, p.57-74

1939 Report on the Animal Remains from Tell-el-Amarna, Upper Egypt. In J. PENDLEBURY The City of Akhenaten, p.247-252, Egypt Exploration Society

1939 Report on the Animal Remains from Further Excavations at Julliberrie's Grave, Chilham. *Antiq. Journal,* XIX, p.278-9

1939 Report on Animal Bones from an Iron Age Hut at Postwick, nr. Norwich. *Norfolk & Norwich Arch. Soc.*, XXVI, p.272-3

1939 Report on Animal Remains from the Excavations at Frilford, Berks. *Oxoniensia,* IV, p.25

1939 Notes on Animal Remains from a Prehistoric Settlement on Walney Island. *Trans. Cumb. & West. Antiq. & Arch. Soc.,* XXXIX, p.277

1939 Report on the Animal Remains from the Iron Age Camp of Briedon Hill, Gloucestershire. *J. R. Archaeol. Inst.,* XCV, p.29 and 40

1939 Discovery of the Remains of the Celtic Short-Horned Ox, *Bos longifrons* Owen, at Whitepark Bay, Co. Antrim. *Irish Nat. Journal,* VII, p.189-192

1939 Report on the Animal Remains found at Quarley Hill, Hampshire. *Proc. Hamps. F.C. and Arch. Soc.,* XIV, p.191-2

1940 Report on Animal Remains from the Late Bronze Age Site at Castle Hill, Newhaven, Sussex. *Sussex Archaeol. Coll.,* LXXX, p.267-8

1941 Report on the Animal Remains from the Bury Hill Excavations, 1939. *Proc. Hamps. F.C. & Arch. Soc.,* XV, p.48-49

1943 Report on Animal Remains from the Late Bronze Age Site at Minnis Bay, Birchington, Kent. *Proc. Prehist. Soc.,* IX, p.41-44

1943 Report on a series of Ox bones from a Late Bronze Age Site on Ogbourne Down near Marlborough. *Ibid.,* VIII, p.54

1943 Report on Animal Bones and Shells from a Late Bronze Age Site at St. Lawrence College, Ramsgate, Kent. *Ibid.,* p.27

1943 Report on Animal Remains from Maiden Castle, Dorset. In R. E. MORTIMER WHEELER, Maiden Castle, p.369-371

1946 Notes on Animal remains found at an Early Iron Age Site at Martinsell, Marlborough. *Wilts. Arch. & Nat. Hist. Mag.,* LI, p.256

1946 Report on a few animal bones from an Iron Age Site at West Clandon. *J.R. Archaeol. Inst.,* CI, p.55

1946 Report on Animal Remains from Pagan Burial Mounds at Ingleby near Repton, Derbyshire. *Derbys. Arch. & Nat. Hist. Soc. Journ.,* XIX, p.22

1947 Mammalian Remains. In C. F. C. HAWKES & M. R. HULL, Camulodunum. First Report on the Excavations at Colchester 1930-1939. *Report Res. Comm. Soc. Antiq. Lond.,* XIV, p.350-354

1947 Report on Animal Remains from the Roman Villa at Park Street, near St. Albans, Herts. *J.R. Archaeol. Inst.,* CII, p.100-102

1948 Notes on Animal Remains from a Romano-British Cremating Place on Roden Downs, Berkshire. *Trans. Newbury Dist. F.Cl.* IX, p.45

1948 Report on the Animal Bones from the Excavations at the Jewry Wall Site, Leicester. *Rep. Res. Comm. Soc. Antiq.,* No. XV, p.285-6

1948 The Animal Remains from Little Woodbury. *Proc. Prehist. Soc.,* XIV, p.19-23

1948 Report on Animal Remains from 'Two Pits of Grooved Ware Date near Woodhenge.' *Wilts. Archaeol. & Nat. Hist. Mag.,* LII, p.300-301

1949 Report on Animal Remains from Wilbury Camp, Herts. *J.R. Archaeol. Inst.*, CVI, p.45

1950 Report on Animal Remains from Breedon-on-the-Hill, Leicestershire. *Trans. Leics. Arch. Soc.*, XXVI, p.17, 43, 73-5

1951 Report on Animal Remains and Shells from the Romano-British Baths at Well, Yorks. *Roman Antiq. Comm. Yorks. Arch. Soc.*, p.63, 64

1957 Report on a Skeleton of an Ox, and Bones from Storage Pit No. 21, Hut C, from a Late Bronze Age Settlement on Itford Hill, Sussex. *Proc. Prehist. Soc.*, XXIII, p.211-212

1961 Report on Animal Remains from Shenbarrow Hill Camp, Stanton, Gloucestershire. *Trans. Bristol & Glouc. Arch. Soc.*, 80, p.37-39

1961 Report on Animal Remains from the Belgic Site at Bagendon, near Cirencester. In E. M. CLIFFORD, Bagendon, p.268-271

ARCHAEOLOGY

1909 On the Diatomaceous Deposit of the Lower Bann Valley, Co.'s Antrim and Derry, and Prehistoric Implements found therein. *Mem. & Proc. Manch. Lit. & Phil. Soc.*, 53, p.1-20, plates I-IV

1914 On the discovery of a Bloomery at Lindale Church, near Grange-over-Sands. *Trans. Cumb. & West. Antiq. & Archaeol. Soc.*, XIV, p.256-261

1915 Dental Mutilations in Neolithic Human Remains. *Journ. Anat. & Physiol., XLIX, p.72-79*

1927 Bronze age find in Cheshire. *Antiq. Journal,* VII, p.62-3

1928 with L. S. PALMER & W. O'B. PIERCE. The Sligo Artefacts. *Nature,* 121, p.501

1928 Flint Adze from Bacup. *Antiq. Journal,* VIII, p.90-91

1930 Early Man in Derbyshire. *Ramblers Federation Handbook,* 15pp

1931 Shale Armlet found near Blackstone Edge. *The Naturalist,* March, p.85-87

1933 Pygmy flint scrapers from Fairhead, Co. Antrim. *Irish Nat. Journal,* IV, p.203

1933 Tanged Flint Point of Bann Type from a Cave at Ballintoy, Co. Antrim. *Ibid.,* p.213-4

1933 Prehistoric Domestic Animals. *Man,* XXXIII, p.87

1934 A Bronze Sword found near Garstang, Lancs. *Antiq. Journal,* XIV, p.179-180

1934 A Figurine from Northern Ireland. *Ibid.,* p. 180-182

1935 The Prehistory of the Manchester Region. *Ancient Monuments Yearbook & Proc.,* p.48-53

1936 The Prehistoric Archaeology of Lancashire and Cheshire. *Trans. Lancs. & Cheshire Antiq. Soc.,* L, 65-106

1936 Contributions to the Archaeology of the Manchester Region. *N. W. Naturalist,* June, 110-119, plate 7 & 8

1937 An Account of a Human Burial on the Shore near Ballintoy Harbour. *Irish Nat. Journal,* VI, p.190-1

1937 Contributions to the Archaeology of the Buxton Region. *N. W. Naturalist,* p.3-7, plates 13-15

1941 A Review of the Neolithic and Bronze Ages of the Buxton District. Reprinted from the *Buxton Advertiser,* March 1, 15, 22, 29, 9pp

1945 A lance-point of Upper Palaeolithic type from Victoria Cave, Settle, Yorkshire. *Antiq. Journal,* XXV, p.147-8, plate XII fig. a

1951 Peterborough (Neolithic B) Pottery from High Wheeldon Cave, Earl Sterndale, near Buxton. *Derbyshire Archaeol. & Nat. Hist. Soc. Journ.,* LXX, p.72-3

1952 Report on Bone Points from the Lower Bann, N. Ireland. *Arch. Res. Publ. N. Ireland,* No. 1, p.15

1963 Terraced Cultivation at Priestcliffe near Taddington. *Derbys. Archaeol. & Nat. Hist. Soc. Journ.* LXXXII, p.100-102, plate VIII

1968 A large Cinerary Urn and Roman Coin found at Glossop. *Ibid.,* LXXXVIII, p.96-7, plate III, fig. b

BIOGRAPHICAL & HISTORICAL

1908 Biography of David Dyson. *Lancs. Naturalist,* I, p.167-170

1925 Obituary Notice: Robert Standen. *J. Conchology,* 17, p.225-235, plate 3

1926 Obituary Notice: John Michael Williams. *Ibid.,* 18, p.9-10

1926 William Henry Heathcote (1861-1926) *North West Naturalist,* June, p.86-88, plate 4

1927 History of the Conchological Society. *J. Conchology,* 18, p.65-70

1929 Obituary. Dr. J. C. Melvill. *Nature,* 124, p.921

1930 Obituary Notice: Dr. J. Cosmo Melvill. *J. Conchology,* 19, p.41-45

1935 Genesis and Progress of the Lancashire and Cheshire Antiquarian Society. *Trans. Lancs. & Cheshire Antiq. Soc.* XLIX, p.104-112

1936 Some Early References to Prehistoric and Roman Antiquities in Lancashire and Cheshire. *Ibid.,* L, p.162-176

1936 Robert John Welch — Reminiscences. *Irish Nat. Journ.,* VI, p.138-40

1937 Obituary Notice: Robert John Welch. *J. Conchology,* 20, p.229-332

1937 A Letter from George Humphrey to William Swainson 1815. *Ibid.,* p.332-337

1940 William Bourke Wright (1876-1939) *N.W. Naturalist,* XV, p.72-75, plate 8

1942 with G. N. RICHARDS. Obituary: C. P. Richards (1851-1941). *J. Conchology,* 21, p.322

1942 Obituary: Bernard Richard Lucas (1864-1941) *Ibid.,* p.322-324

1943 Obituary: Walter Medley Tattersall (1882-1943) *N.W. Naturalist,* Dec., p.328-330

1944 Biography of Captain Thomas Brown (1785-1862) a former Curator of the Manchester Museum. *Mem. & Proc. Manch. Lit. & Phil. Soc.,* 86, p.1-28

1945 Martin Lister and Yorkshire Geology and Conchology. *The Naturalist,* Jan.-March, p.1-10

1946 George Cooper Spence. *J. Conchology,* 22, p.206-7

1946 A further note on Martin Lister, with reference to *Ammonites reniformis* Bruguière. *The Naturalist,* July-Sept., p.100

1946 The Lancashire and Cheshire Antiquarian Society, 1883-1943. *Trans. Lancs. & Cheshire Antiq. Soc.,* LVII, p.1-17, plates I-XXII

1949 Obituary. C. H. Moore, 1869-1949. *J. Conchology,* 23, p.85-90

1950 A Retrospect of Twenty-Five Years (1925-1950). *J. Manch. Geol. Assn.,* II, p.51-60

1950 Obituary. W. Thurgood. 1876-1948. *J. Conchology,* 23, p.119-120

1963 with N. F. McMILLAN. Joseph Wilcock of Wakefield and his publications. *Ibid.,* 25, p.201

1966 Sir William Boyd Dawkins (1837-1929) A Biographical Sketch. *Cave Science,* 5, p.398-412, 2 plates

1972 Obituary. William Ernest Alkins (1896-1969) *J. Conchology,* 27, p.432-3

MISCELLANEOUS

1905 High Tides in Morecambe Bay. *The Naturalist,* No. 587, p.373-375

1915 Notes on Degeneration in the teeth of Oxen and Sheep. *Ann. Mag. Nat. Hist.,* XV, p.291-295

1919 The bristly millipede at Saltwick Bay, near Whitby. *The Naturalist,* July, p.243-4

1934 Discovery of encrusing alga *(Hildenbranchia rivuleris)* in stones in the River Bann, N. Ireland. *Irish Nat. Journ.,* V, p.83

1944 Presidential Address. N.W. Federation of Museums and Art Galleries, p.9-22